UNDERSTANDING YOUR POTENTIAL

Dr. Maxwell Shimba

Printed by Shimba Publishing LLC
Printed in the United States of America

TABLE OF CONTENTS

Introduction v

Chapter 01 1

The Biblical Foundation of Potential 1

    Created in God's Image 6

    The Parable of the Talents 11

    Jeremiah's Calling 17

Chapter 02 22

Historical Figures Who Realized Their Potential 22

    2.1 Moses: From Shepherd to Leader 22

    2.2 Esther: Courage and Influence 27

    2.3 Martin Luther King Jr.: A Modern-Day Prophet 32

Chapter 03 39

Unlocking Your Potential 39

    3.1 Self-Discovery and Reflection 45

    3.2 Seeking God's Guidance 52

    3.3 Overcoming Obstacles 57

Chapter 04 65

Cultivating Potenital in Others 65

    4.1 Mentorship and Encouragement 65

    4.2 Building a Supportive Community 71

    4.3 Theological Perspective on Building a Supportive Community
    77

    4.4 Empowering Through Education 83

Chapter 05..**91**

The Legacy of Realized Potential..**91**

5.1 Biblical Legacies 91

5.2 Historical Legacies 98

5.3 Your Legacy 104

Conclusion... **111**

Appendices **115**

Appendix A, B, C, and D **115**

Appendix A: Key Biblical Verses on Potential and Legacy 115

Appendix B: Key Historical Figures and Their Contributions..... 117

Appendix C: Practical Steps for Realizing Potential 118

Appendix D: Reflective Questions for Personal Growth............. 119

INTRODUCTION

Understanding Your Potential

The concept of potential is deeply rooted in both scripture and history. Throughout the Bible, numerous figures have unlocked their potential, demonstrating that every individual possesses innate capabilities given by God. This book aims to explore the biblical foundation of human potential and examine historical examples of individuals who have realized their God-given abilities.

In every human heart lies a desire to fulfill a greater purpose, a calling that goes beyond the mundane routines of daily life. This yearning is not a mere coincidence but a divine implant, a spark of the Creator's image within us. As we embark on this journey to understand our potential, it is crucial to recognize that this potential is not self-generated but is a gift from God.

In Genesis 1:27, we read, "So God created mankind in his own image, in the image of God he created them; male and female he created them." This passage highlights a profound truth: being created in God's image endows us with unique qualities and capabilities. It implies that we carry a fragment of the divine within us, equipping us with the potential for creativity, leadership, compassion, and transformation.

The Bible is replete with narratives of individuals who, despite their initial weaknesses or obscure beginnings, rose to fulfill extraordinary destinies. These stories are not just historical accounts but divine revelations intended to inspire and guide us. For example, Moses, a man with a speech impediment, became the leader who delivered Israel from bondage (Exodus 4:10-12). Similarly, David, a shepherd boy, was anointed to become a king whose lineage would lead to the Messiah (1 Samuel 16:11-13).

Jesus Christ himself embodies the ultimate realization of potential. Born in humble circumstances, he lived a life that transformed the world. His ministry, teachings, sacrifice, and resurrection reveal the fullness of human potential when aligned with God's purpose. In John 14:12, Jesus declares, "Very truly I tell you, whoever believes in me will do the works I have been doing, and they will do even greater things than these, because I am going to the Father." This promise is a testament to the extraordinary potential within each believer.

Historical evidence further supports the biblical understanding of potential. Throughout history, individuals who tapped into their God-given abilities have shaped civilizations, advanced knowledge, and championed justice. Figures such as Martin Luther King Jr., whose vision and courage propelled the civil rights movement, demonstrate how faith and purpose can lead to transformative impact.

As we delve deeper into this book, we will explore the biblical foundations of potential, examining key scriptural passages and the lives of pivotal biblical figures. We will also look at historical examples of individuals who have realized their potential, drawing lessons that are applicable to our own lives.

Understanding your potential is not merely an intellectual exercise but a spiritual awakening. It involves recognizing the divine imprint within you and aligning your life with God's purposes. It requires faith, perseverance, and a willingness to step into the unknown, trusting that God's plans for you are good (Jeremiah 29:11).

This book, "Understanding Your Potential," is an invitation to embark on a transformative journey. It is an invitation to discover the greatness within you, to unlock the divine capabilities bestowed upon you, and to fulfill the unique purpose for which you were created. As you read through these pages, may you be inspired, challenged, and equipped to realize your full potential, bringing glory to God and making a lasting impact on the world.

DR. MAXWELL SHIMBA

CHAPTER 01

THE BIBLICAL FOUNDATION OF POTENTIAL

1.0 What is the Theological Meaning of Potential

The concept of potential from a theological perspective is profoundly intertwined with the nature of God and His creation. Potential, in this sense, is not merely about personal achievement or success but about fulfilling the purpose for which God has created each individual. Understanding potential theologically requires us to delve into the nature of God, the image of God in humanity, and the divine purposes embedded within us.

1.1 Created in the Image of God

The foundation of human potential lies in the doctrine of Imago Dei, which means "image of God." Genesis 1:26-27 states, "Then God said, 'Let us make mankind in our image, in our likeness... So God created mankind in his own image, in the image of God he created them; male and female he created them.'" This passage reveals that humans are unique among creation, endowed with attributes that reflect God's own nature.

Being created in the image of God implies that we possess certain divine qualities: rationality, creativity, relationality, and moral capacity. These qualities are the bedrock of our potential. They signify that every human being has the inherent ability to think, create, relate, and choose in ways that mirror God's character. Our potential is, therefore, a reflection of God's attributes in us.

1.2 Potential as Divine Calling

Potential is also understood as a divine calling. Each person is created with a specific purpose and calling that aligns with God's greater plan. Ephesians 2:10 articulates this truth: "For we are God's handiwork, created in Christ Jesus to do good works, which God prepared in advance for us to do." This verse highlights that our potential is intricately linked to the good works God has prepared for us.

Theological potential is not just about what we can achieve but about fulfilling the roles and tasks God has designed for us. It's about being faithful stewards of the gifts, talents, and opportunities God has entrusted to us. This stewardship is evident in the Parable of the Talents (Matthew 25:14-30), where servants are given talents (a form of currency) to manage. Those who invest and multiply their talents are rewarded, while the one who buries his talent is reprimanded. This parable illustrates that God expects us to develop and use our abilities for His kingdom purposes.

1.3 The Role of the Holy Spirit

The Holy Spirit plays a crucial role in realizing our potential. The Spirit empowers believers to fulfill their divine calling and to grow into the likeness of Christ. Acts 1:8 promises, "But you will receive power when the Holy Spirit comes on you; and you will be my witnesses in Jerusalem, and in all Judea and Samaria, and to the ends of the earth."

The Holy Spirit's empowerment is essential for unlocking our potential. It is through the Spirit that we receive spiritual gifts (1 Corinthians 12:4-11), guidance, and strength to live out our calling. The Spirit works within us to transform our character, align our desires with God's will, and equip us for service. Therefore, our potential is not realized in our own strength but through the enabling power of the Holy Spirit.

1.4 The Example of Jesus Christ

Jesus Christ serves as the ultimate example of realized potential. Though fully divine, Jesus lived a fully human life, demonstrating what it means to live in perfect alignment with God's will. Philippians 2:6-8 describes Jesus' humility and obedience: "Who, being in very nature God, did not consider equality with God something to be used to his own advantage; rather, he made himself nothing by taking the very nature of a servant, being made in human likeness. And being found in appearance as a man, he humbled himself by becoming obedient to death—even death on a cross!"

Jesus' life, ministry, death, and resurrection exemplify the fulfillment of divine potential. He perfectly manifested God's love, justice, mercy, and truth. In doing so, He set a pattern for believers to follow. Jesus' statement in John 14:12, "Very truly I tell you, whoever believes in me will do the works I have been doing, and they will do even greater things than these, because I am going to the Father," indicates that believers are called to continue His work and, empowered by the Holy Spirit, to realize their potential in advancing God's kingdom.

1.5 The Eschatological Perspective

From an eschatological perspective, potential is also linked to the ultimate fulfillment of God's plan for creation. Romans 8:19-21 speaks of creation's longing for the revelation of the children of God: "For the creation waits in eager expectation for the children of God to be revealed. For the creation was subjected to frustration, not by its own choice, but by the will of the one who subjected it, in hope that the creation itself will be liberated from its bondage to decay and brought into the freedom and glory of the children of God."

This passage suggests that the realization of human potential is part of the broader redemption and restoration of creation. As we grow into our potential, we participate in God's redemptive work, moving towards the final restoration of all things.

The theological meaning of potential is deeply rooted in the nature of God and His purposes for humanity. It is about being created in God's image, fulfilling our divine calling, being empowered by the Holy Spirit, following the example of Jesus Christ, and participating in God's redemptive plan for creation. Understanding and realizing our potential is a spiritual journey that requires faith, obedience, and reliance on God's grace and power. As we embrace this journey, we discover the fullness of life that God intends for us, bringing glory to Him and advancing His kingdom on earth.

Created in God's Image

1.1 Created in God's Image

The concept of being created in God's image, or Imago Dei, is one of the most profound truths found in the Bible. It sets the foundation for understanding human dignity, worth, and potential. This chapter will delve into the theological significance of Imago Dei, using biblical teachings and comprehensive commentary supported by exhaustive references from Strong's Concordance.

1.1.1 Theological Significance of Imago Dei

Genesis 1:27 (NIV) states, "So God created mankind in his own image, in the image of God he created them; male and female he created them." The phrase "image of God" (tselem Elohim) is crucial for understanding our potential. According to Strong's Concordance (H6754), tselem means a resemblance or a representative figure. This implies that humans are not only similar to God in some respects but also represent Him on earth.

1.1.2 Unique Abilities and Creativity

Being created in God's image endows humans with unique abilities and creativity. God, the ultimate Creator, has imparted a portion of His creative power to humanity. This is evident in our ability to imagine, design, and innovate. Ecclesiastes 3:11 (NIV) states, "He has made everything beautiful in its time. He has also set eternity in the human heart; yet no one can fathom what God has done from beginning to end." The phrase "set eternity in the human heart" suggests a divine curiosity and a drive to explore beyond the immediate and the mundane.

1.1.3 Capacity for Relationships

One of the most significant aspects of being made in God's image is our capacity for relationships. God is inherently relational, existing eternally as Father, Son, and Holy Spirit. This relational aspect is reflected in humanity's need and ability to form meaningful relationships. Genesis 2:18 (NIV) says, "The Lord God said, 'It is not good for the man to be alone. I will make a helper suitable for him.'" The creation of Eve from Adam underscores the importance of companionship and community.

1.1.4 Moral Capacity

Humans, being in God's image, possess a moral capacity that sets them apart from the rest of creation. This moral awareness is a reflection of God's own holiness and justice. Romans 2:14-15 (NIV) states, "(Indeed, when Gentiles, who do not have the law, do by nature things required by the law, they are a law for themselves, even though they do not have the law. They show that the requirements of the law are written on their hearts, their consciences also bearing witness, and their thoughts sometimes accusing them and at other times even defending them.)" This passage illustrates that the moral law is inherent in human nature, pointing to our divine origin.

1.1.5 Stewardship and Dominion

Another aspect of Imago Dei is the mandate to exercise stewardship and dominion over creation. Genesis 1:28 (NIV) says, "God blessed them and said to them, 'Be fruitful and increase in number; fill the earth and subdue it. Rule over the fish in the sea and the birds in the sky and over every living creature that moves on the ground.'" The terms "subdue" (kabash, H3533) and "rule" (radah, H7287) in Strong's Concordance convey a sense of responsibility and care, not exploitation. Humans are called to manage the earth's resources wisely, reflecting God's sovereign care.

1.1.6 Redemption and Restoration

The fall of humanity marred the image of God within us, but it did not erase it. The redemptive work of Christ aims to restore the fullness of Imago Dei in us. Colossians 3:10 (NIV) states, "and have put on the new self, which is being renewed in knowledge in the image of its Creator." Through Christ, we are being transformed into the likeness of God, fulfilling our true potential. Ephesians 4:24 (NIV) also emphasizes this renewal: "and to put on the new self, created to be like God in true righteousness and holiness."

1.1.7 The Eschatological Perspective

Ultimately, the restoration of God's image in humanity will be completed in the eschaton. 1 John 3:2 (NIV) declares, "Dear friends, now we are children of God, and what we will be has not yet been made known. But we know that when Christ appears, we shall be like him, for we shall see him as he is." This future hope points to the full realization of our potential as bearers of God's image.

Comprehensive Commentary

Genesis 1:27: The creation account in Genesis emphasizes the uniqueness of humans. The Hebrew term tselem is used to denote an image or likeness, suggesting a resemblance that is more than physical. Theologians have long debated what aspects of humanity reflect God's image, often pointing to intellectual, moral, relational, and spiritual capacities.

Ecclesiastes 3:11: This verse highlights the innate human longing for understanding and purpose, which is a reflection of God's infinite wisdom. The term olam (H5769), translated as "eternity," indicates an indefinite, unending period, suggesting that humans are created with a sense of the eternal and the divine.

Genesis 2:18: The relational aspect of humanity is crucial. The term ezer (H5828), translated as "helper," signifies one who provides essential support, reflecting the communal nature of the Godhead.

Romans 2:14-15: This passage speaks to the innate moral consciousness within humans. The Greek term syneidesis (G4893), translated as "conscience," indicates an internal awareness of right and wrong, underscoring the divine moral imprint in humanity.

Genesis 1:28: The mandate to "subdue" and "rule" over creation is significant. The term kabash implies bringing under control, while radah suggests governing with authority. This stewardship reflects God's sovereign rule and entrusts humanity with the care of His creation.

Colossians 3:10: The renewal in the image of the Creator is a key aspect of Christian sanctification. The Greek term anakainoo (G341) means to make new, indicating a continuous process of transformation into the likeness of God.

1 John 3:2: This eschatological promise assures believers of their future transformation. The term phaino (G5316), translated as "appears," signifies a visible manifestation, pointing to the ultimate revelation and realization of our divine potential.

Being created in God's image is foundational to understanding human potential. It implies that we are endowed with unique abilities, creativity, relational capacity, and moral awareness. The biblical mandate to steward creation and the promise of redemption and restoration through Christ further emphasize our divine potential. By comprehensively exploring these themes with the aid of Strong's Concordance, we gain a deeper appreciation of what it means to be made in the image of God and how this shapes our understanding of potential.

The Parable of the Talents

1.2 The Parable of the Talents

The Parable of the Talents, found in Matthew 25:14-30, is a profound teaching by Jesus that highlights the importance of recognizing and utilizing the gifts and abilities that God has entrusted to us. This chapter will explore the theological and practical implications of this parable, supported by comprehensive biblical commentary and exhaustive references from Strong's Concordance.

1.2.1 Understanding the Parable

Matthew 25:14-30 (NIV) states:

> "Again, it will be like a man going on a journey, who called his servants and entrusted his wealth to them. To one he gave five bags of gold, to another two bags, and to another one bag, each according to his ability. Then he went on his journey. The man who had received five bags of gold went at

once and put his money to work and gained five bags more. So also, the one with two bags of gold gained two more. But the man who had received one bag went off, dug a hole in the ground and hid his master's money.

> "After a long time the master of those servants returned and settled accounts with them. The man who had received five bags of gold brought the other five. 'Master,' he said, 'you entrusted me with five bags of gold. See, I have gained five more.'

> "His master replied, 'Well done, good and faithful servant! You have been faithful with a few things; I will put you in charge of many things. Come and share your master's happiness!'

> "The man with two bags of gold also came. 'Master,' he said, 'you entrusted me with two bags of gold; see, I have gained two more.'

> "His master replied, 'Well done, good and faithful servant! You have been faithful with a few things; I will put you in charge of many things. Come and share your master's happiness!'

> "Then the man who had received one bag of gold came. 'Master,' he said, 'I knew that you are a hard man, harvesting where you have not sown and gathering where you have not scattered seed. So I was afraid and went out and hid your gold in the ground. See, here is what belongs to you.'

> "His master replied, 'You wicked, lazy servant! So you knew that I harvest where I have not sown and gather where I have not scattered seed? Well then, you should have put my money on deposit with the bankers, so that when I returned I would have received it back with interest.

> "'So take the bag of gold from him and give it to the one who has ten bags. For whoever has will be given more, and they will have an abundance. Whoever does not have, even what they have will be taken from them. And throw that worthless servant outside, into the darkness, where there will be weeping and gnashing of teeth.'"

1.2.2 Theological Implications

The parable is rich with theological significance. The "man going on a journey" represents Christ, who has ascended into heaven and will return to judge humanity. The "servants" symbolize believers who are entrusted with various gifts, abilities, and opportunities. The "talents" (talanta, G5007) represent the resources, gifts, and responsibilities given by God.

1.2.3 The Principle of Stewardship

The parable emphasizes the principle of stewardship. Each servant is given a different amount of talents, "each according to his ability" (Matthew 25:15). The Greek word for ability is dynamis (G1411), which denotes power or capability.

This suggests that God entrusts resources to individuals based on their capacity to manage them.

1 Peter 4:10 (NIV) reinforces this idea: "Each of you should use whatever gift you have received to serve others, as faithful stewards of God's grace in its various forms." This verse highlights that our gifts are to be used in service to others, reflecting God's grace.

1.2.4 The Rewards of Faithfulness

The servants who invested their talents were rewarded. The master's response, "Well done, good and faithful servant!" (Matthew 25:21, 23), underscores the value of faithfulness. The Greek word for faithful is pistos (G4103), meaning trustworthy or reliable. Faithfulness in small matters leads to greater responsibilities and blessings, as seen in Luke 16:10 (NIV): "Whoever can be trusted with very little can also be trusted with much."

1.2.5 The Consequences of Neglect

The servant who hid his talent faced severe consequences. His actions, driven by fear and misperception of the master's character, resulted in his punishment. The master's rebuke, "You wicked, lazy servant!" (Matthew 25:26), uses the Greek words poneros (G4190) for wicked, meaning evil or morally corrupt, and okneros (G3636) for lazy, meaning idle or slothful.

This underscores the dangers of neglecting our God-given gifts. James 4:17 (NIV) warns, "If anyone, then, knows the good they ought to do and doesn't do it, it is sin for them." Failure to utilize our potential is viewed as a moral failing.

1.2.6 The Principle of Increase

The principle of increase is evident in the master's command to take the talent from the unfaithful servant and give it to the one with ten talents. Matthew 25:29 (NIV) states, "For whoever has will be given more, and they will have an abundance. Whoever does not have, even what they have will be taken from them." This principle, also seen in Luke 19:26, indicates that diligent and faithful use of resources leads to greater abundance.

Comprehensive Commentary

Matthew 25:14-30: The context of this parable is Jesus' teaching on the Kingdom of Heaven. The talents (talanta, G5007) are significant amounts of money, symbolizing substantial resources or responsibilities. The master's journey represents Christ's ascension and anticipated return.

Matthew 25:15: The term dynamis (G1411) for ability highlights that God's distribution of gifts is based on His knowledge of our capacities. This aligns with 1 Corinthians

12:7-11, where spiritual gifts are distributed by the Holy Spirit as He wills.

Matthew 25:21, 23: The commendation "Well done, good and faithful servant" uses pistos (G4103), emphasizing the value God places on reliability and integrity in stewardship. This is further supported by 1 Corinthians 4:2 (NIV): "Now it is required that those who have been given a trust must prove faithful."

Matthew 25:26: The terms poneros (G4190) and okneros (G3636) convey strong disapproval of the servant's actions. These words reflect the moral and ethical implications of failing to utilize one's potential, aligning with the broader biblical theme of diligence and responsibility (Proverbs 10:4, Romans 12:11).

Matthew 25:29: The principle of increase is a recurring biblical theme. Proverbs 11:24-25 (NIV) states, "One person gives freely, yet gains even more; another withholds unduly, but comes to poverty. A generous person will prosper; whoever refreshes others will be refreshed." This principle encourages faithful and generous use of God's gifts.

The Parable of the Talents offers profound insights into the importance of recognizing and utilizing our God-given gifts. It underscores the principles of stewardship, faithfulness, and the consequences of neglect. By exploring this parable through comprehensive biblical commentary and references from Strong's Concordance, we gain a deeper understanding of our responsibilities as stewards of God's resources. Embracing these truths encourages us to faithfully invest our talents for God's glory and the advancement of His Kingdom.

Jeremiah's Calling

1.3 Jeremiah's Calling

The calling of Jeremiah offers profound insights into the nature of divine purpose and human potential. Jeremiah 1:5 encapsulates God's preordained plan for Jeremiah, highlighting the belief that our potential and purpose are intricately woven into the fabric of our being, even before birth. This chapter will explore the theological significance of Jeremiah's calling, supported by comprehensive biblical teachings and exhaustive references from Strong's Concordance.

1.3.1 Divine Foreknowledge and Preordination

Jeremiah 1:5 (NIV) states, "Before I formed you in the womb I knew you, before you were born I set you apart; I appointed you as a prophet to the nations." The term "knew" (yada, H3045) signifies an intimate and comprehensive knowledge. This indicates that God's relationship with

Jeremiah—and by extension, with each of us—begins even before our physical formation.

1.3.2 Set Apart for a Purpose

The phrase "set you apart" uses the Hebrew word qadash (H6942), which means to consecrate or sanctify. This denotes a special purpose and a sacred calling. In Jeremiah's case, it was to be a prophet to the nations. This preordination emphasizes that God has a specific plan for each individual, imbued with purpose and potential.

1.3.3 Appointed by God

The word "appointed" (natan, H5414) means to give, put, or set. In this context, it implies a divine assignment. Jeremiah was given the role of a prophet, not by his own choosing but by God's sovereign will. This appointment underscores the belief that our callings are divinely ordained and not merely the result of personal ambition.

1.3.4 Jeremiah's Initial Hesitation

Jeremiah's response to God's call was one of hesitation and self-doubt. Jeremiah 1:6 (NIV) records his reaction: "Alas, Sovereign Lord, I do not know how to speak; I am too young." The term "alas" (ahah, H162) expresses a deep emotional lament. This reveals Jeremiah's fear and perceived inadequacy, common reactions to divine callings.

1.3.5 God's Reassurance

In response to Jeremiah's hesitation, God offers reassurance. Jeremiah 1:7-8 (NIV) states, "But the Lord said to me, 'Do not say, 'I am too young.' You must go to everyone I send you to and say whatever I command you. Do not be afraid of them, for I am with you and will rescue you,' declares the Lord." The promise of God's presence (anoki, H595) and rescue (natsal, H5337) provides the assurance needed to fulfill his calling.

1.3.6 Divine Empowerment

Jeremiah 1:9 (NIV) describes God's empowerment: "Then the Lord reached out his hand and touched my mouth and said to me, 'I have put my words in your mouth.'" The act of touching (naga, H5060) symbolizes impartation of power and authority. God's words (dabar, H1697) in Jeremiah's mouth signify divine inspiration and guidance.

1.3.7 The Scope of Jeremiah's Mission

Jeremiah's mission was extensive and challenging. Jeremiah 1:10 (NIV) states, "See, today I appoint you over nations and kingdoms to uproot and tear down, to destroy and overthrow, to build and to plant." The verbs used— uproot (nathash, H5428), tear down (nathats, H5422), destroy (abad, H6), overthrow (haras, H2040), build (banah, H1129), and plant (nata, H5193)—reflect a comprehensive mission involving judgment and restoration.

Comprehensive Commentary

Jeremiah 1:5: The phrase "I knew you" (yada, H3045) implies an intimate knowledge, signifying God's deep understanding and intentionality. This foreknowledge is echoed in Psalm 139:13-16, which celebrates God's intricate involvement in our formation.

Jeremiah 1:6: Jeremiah's expression of inadequacy reflects a common theme in biblical call narratives, such as Moses' reluctance in Exodus 4:10 and Isaiah's in Isaiah 6:5. The term "too young" (na'ar, H5288) indicates youth and inexperience, highlighting the divine preference for using seemingly unqualified individuals.

Jeremiah 1:7-8: God's reassurance to Jeremiah is paralleled in Joshua 1:9, where God commands, "Be strong and courageous. Do not be afraid; do not be discouraged, for the Lord your God will be with you wherever you go." The promise of God's presence (anoki, H595) is a central theme in biblical assurances.

Jeremiah 1:9: The act of touching Jeremiah's mouth (naga, H5060) is significant, indicating divine impartation. Similar acts of divine touch are seen in Isaiah 6:7 and Ezekiel 3:1-3, symbolizing empowerment and purification.

Jeremiah 1:10: The comprehensive nature of Jeremiah's mission is reflected in the verbs used. These actions—uproot (nathash, H5428), tear down (nathats,

H5422), destroy (abad, H6), overthrow (haras, H2040), build (banah, H1129), and plant (nata, H5193)—illustrate the dual aspects of prophetic ministry: judgment and restoration. These themes are recurrent throughout Jeremiah's ministry and are central to the prophetic literature.

1.3.8 The Relevance of Jeremiah's Calling Today

Jeremiah's calling is not just a historical account but a source of inspiration for contemporary believers. It emphasizes that each person's potential and purpose are known by God from the beginning. This calling requires courage, reliance on God's presence, and willingness to embrace both the challenges and opportunities that come with fulfilling our divine purpose.

Jeremiah's calling illustrates the profound truth that our potential and purpose are preordained by God. Despite initial fears and perceived inadequacies, Jeremiah's life demonstrates the importance of trusting in God's plan, receiving His empowerment, and embracing our divine assignments. By exploring Jeremiah's calling through comprehensive biblical teachings and references from Strong's Concordance, we gain deeper insights into how we, too, can recognize and fulfill our God-given potential.

CHAPTER 02

HISTORICAL FIGURES WHO REALIZED THEIR POTENTIAL

2.1 Moses: From Shepherd to Leader

Moses is one of the most prominent figures in the Bible, whose life journey from a humble shepherd to the leader of the Israelites exemplifies the realization of one's potential. His story is a powerful illustration of how God can transform and use seemingly ordinary individuals for extraordinary purposes. This chapter explores Moses' life, his initial hesitations, and his ultimate acceptance of his divine calling, supported by comprehensive biblical teachings and references from Strong's Concordance.

2.1.1 Early Life and Background

Moses' early life is marked by dramatic events that set the stage for his future role. Born to Hebrew parents during a time of severe oppression under Pharaoh, Moses was miraculously saved from infanticide and raised in Pharaoh's household (Exodus 2:1-10). This dual heritage provided him with a unique perspective and preparation for his future leadership.

2.1.2 Moses' Hesitation and God's Call

Moses' initial encounter with God at the burning bush is a turning point in his life. Exodus 3:1-10 describes this divine encounter, where God calls Moses to deliver the Israelites from slavery. Moses' response reveals his self-doubt and reluctance. Exodus 3:11 (NIV) states, "But Moses said to God, 'Who am I that I should go to Pharaoh and bring the Israelites out of Egypt?'" The phrase "Who am I" (miy anokhi, H4310 and H595) reflects Moses' deep sense of inadequacy.

2.1.3 God's Reassurance and Empowerment

Despite Moses' hesitations, God provides reassurance and promises His presence. Exodus 3:12 (NIV) records, "And God said, 'I will be with you. And this will be the sign to you that it is I who have sent you: When you have brought the people out of Egypt, you will worship God on this mountain.'" The assurance "I will be with you" (anokhi eheyeh imak, H595 and H1961) emphasizes God's continuous presence and support.

2.1.4 The Significance of God's Name

In Exodus 3:14, God reveals His name to Moses: "God said to Moses, 'I AM WHO I AM. This is what you are to say to the Israelites: I AM has sent me to you.'" The term "I AM" (ehyeh asher ehyeh, H1961 and H834) signifies God's eternal, self-sustaining existence, providing Moses with the confidence to trust in God's unchanging nature.

2.1.5 Moses' Transformation through Obedience

As Moses begins to obey God's commands, his transformation from a hesitant shepherd to a decisive leader becomes evident. This transformation is marked by key events, including the confrontation with Pharaoh, the ten plagues, and the parting of the Red Sea (Exodus 7-14). Each event demonstrates Moses' growing faith and leadership.

2.1.6 Receiving the Ten Commandments

One of the most significant moments in Moses' leadership journey is receiving the Ten Commandments on Mount Sinai. Exodus 19:3 (NIV) describes Moses' ascent: "Then Moses went up to God, and the Lord called to him from the mountain and said, 'This is what you are to say to the descendants of Jacob and what you are to tell the people of Israel.'" The giving of the Law established Moses as the mediator between God and Israel, solidifying his role as leader and lawgiver.

Comprehensive Commentary

Exodus 3:11: Moses' question "Who am I" (miy anokhi, H4310 and H595) highlights his humility and self-doubt. This sentiment is echoed in other biblical figures who felt inadequate for their divine calling, such as Gideon (Judges 6:15) and Jeremiah (Jeremiah 1:6).

Exodus 3:12: The assurance "I will be with you" (anokhi eheyeh imak, H595 and H1961) is a recurring promise in the Bible, signifying God's constant presence and support. This is also seen in God's assurances to Joshua (Joshua 1:5) and the disciples (Matthew 28:20).

Exodus 3:14: The revelation of God's name "I AM" (ehyeh asher ehyeh, H1961 and H834) signifies His self-existence and eternal nature. This foundational truth is further expounded in John 8:58, where Jesus declares, "Before Abraham was born, I am," linking His identity with the eternal God.

Exodus 19:3: Moses' role as a mediator is crucial, as he conveys God's laws and covenant to the Israelites. This mediatorial role is a foreshadowing of Christ's ultimate mediation between God and humanity (1 Timothy 2:5).

2.1.7 Lessons from Moses' Leadership

Moses' journey offers several key lessons for realizing our potential:

1. Humility and Reliance on God: Moses' initial reluctance and humility are crucial for leadership. True potential is realized not through self-reliance but through dependence on God.

2. Obedience to God's Call: Despite his fears, Moses' obedience to God's call leads to his transformation and effectiveness as a leader.

3. Trust in God's Promises: God's repeated assurances of His presence and power provide the foundation for Moses' confidence and success.

4. Perseverance through Challenges: Moses' perseverance through numerous challenges, including opposition from Pharaoh and complaints from the Israelites, highlights the importance of steadfastness in fulfilling one's divine calling.

2.1.8 Relevance for Today

Moses' story remains relevant for contemporary believers. It teaches that:

- God's Calling Transcends Our Limitations: Our perceived inadequacies do not disqualify us from God's service. God equips those He calls.

- Divine Purpose: Each person has a unique role in God's plan, and realizing this potential requires faith and obedience.

- Leadership and Service: True leadership in God's kingdom is marked by humility, service, and reliance on God's guidance.

Moses' transformation from a shepherd to the leader of the Israelites exemplifies the realization of divine potential. His journey, marked by initial hesitation, divine reassurance, and ultimate obedience, serves as a powerful example of how God can use ordinary individuals for extraordinary purposes. By exploring Moses' life through comprehensive biblical teachings and references from Strong's Concordance, we gain deeper insights into the principles of humility, obedience, and trust that are essential for realizing our potential.

2.2 Esther: Courage and Influence

Esther, a Jewish queen in Persia, stands as a testament to the power of courage and influence. Her story is a compelling narrative of how one individual, recognizing and acting upon her potential, can change the course of history. This chapter explores Esther's journey, her moment of decision, and the impact of her actions, supported by comprehensive biblical teachings and references from Strong's Concordance.

2.2.1 Esther's Background and Rise to Queenship

Esther's story begins with her humble beginnings as Hadassah, an orphaned Jewish girl raised by her cousin Mordecai (Esther 2:7). She rises to prominence when King Xerxes of Persia chooses her as queen, unaware of her Jewish heritage (Esther 2:17). This elevation places Esther in a unique position of influence.

2.2.2 The Threat to the Jewish People

The central crisis in the Book of Esther is the plot by Haman, an advisor to King Xerxes, to annihilate all Jews in the Persian Empire. Haman's hatred for Mordecai, who refused to bow to him, fuels his genocidal scheme (Esther 3:5-6). The decree to destroy the Jews is sealed with the king's signet ring, making it irrevocable (Esther 3:12-13).

2.2.3 Mordecai's Appeal to Esther

Mordecai's plea to Esther to intervene is a pivotal moment. Esther 4:13-14 (NIV) records Mordecai's words: "Do not think that because you are in the king's house you alone of all the Jews will escape. For if you remain silent at this time, relief and deliverance for the Jews will arise from another place, but you and your father's family will perish. And who knows but that you have come to your royal position for such a time as this?" The phrase "for such a time as this" (et ka-zot higatta, H6256 and H5060) underscores the divine timing and purpose of Esther's position.

2.2.4 Esther's Decision and Preparation

Esther's courageous decision to approach the king, despite the law that anyone who approached the king without being summoned could be put to death (Esther 4:11), marks the climax of her story. Esther 4:16 (NIV) records her resolve: "Go, gather together all the Jews who are in Susa, and fast for me. Do not eat or drink for three days, night or day. I and my attendants will fast as you do. When this is done, I will go to the king, even though it is against the law. And if I perish, I perish." The term "perish" (abad, H6) indicates the gravity of the risk she was willing to take.

2.2.5 Esther's Influence and God's Providence

Esther's approach to the king results in a favorable reception. Her courage and wisdom in planning the banquets (Esther 5:1-8) and revealing Haman's plot (Esther 7:3-6) lead to Haman's downfall and the king's decree allowing the Jews to defend themselves (Esther 8:11). Esther's actions demonstrate the profound influence she wielded and the providence of God in delivering His people.

Comprehensive Commentary

Esther 2:7: The mention of Esther's Hebrew name Hadassah (Hadaccah, H1919) signifies her Jewish identity, which she later reveals at a critical moment. The name Esther (Ecter, H635) means "star," reflecting her rise to prominence.

Esther 3:12-13: The decree issued by Haman, sealed with the king's signet ring, indicates the irrevocable nature of Persian law (dat, H1881). This sets the stage for the dramatic reversal that follows.

Esther 4:13-14: Mordecai's appeal to Esther highlights the concept of divine timing and purpose. The term "relief and deliverance" (revach ve-hatzalah, H7305 and H3444) signifies the hope of salvation, whether through Esther or another means, reflecting God's sovereignty.

Esther 4:16: Esther's call for fasting (tzom, H6685) aligns with the Jewish practice of seeking God's intervention. Her statement "If I perish, I perish" demonstrates her acceptance of potential martyrdom, akin to the resolve shown by other biblical figures like Daniel (Daniel 3:16-18).

Esther 5:1-8: Esther's strategic planning in inviting the king and Haman to banquets displays her wisdom and tact. This approach allows her to gain favor and set the stage for revealing Haman's plot.

Esther 7:3-6: Esther's bold revelation of her Jewish identity and Haman's plot highlights her courage. The term "enemy" (tsar, H6862) used to describe Haman emphasizes the personal and national threat he posed.

2.2.6 Lessons from Esther's Courage and Influence

Esther's story offers several key lessons for realizing our potential:

1. Courage in Adversity: Esther's willingness to risk her life for her people exemplifies the courage needed to fulfill one's purpose.

2. Recognizing Divine Timing: The phrase "for such a time as this" underscores the importance of recognizing and seizing the moments God provides.

3. Wisdom and Strategy: Esther's careful planning and execution of her strategy demonstrate the importance of wisdom in leadership.

4. Faith and Dependence on God: Esther's call for fasting highlights the need for spiritual preparation and reliance on God's intervention.

2.2.7 Relevance for Today

Esther's story remains relevant for contemporary believers. It teaches that:

- God Places Us in Strategic Positions: Our roles and positions are often divinely orchestrated for specific purposes.

- Individual Actions Can Make a Difference: One person's courage and faith can have a profound impact on a larger community.

- Trust in God's Sovereignty: God's providence is at work, even in seemingly dire circumstances.

Esther's journey from a Jewish orphan to the queen of Persia exemplifies the power of courage and influence. Her story demonstrates how recognizing and acting upon one's potential can lead to significant and positive changes. By exploring Esther's life through comprehensive biblical teachings and references from Strong's Concordance, we gain deeper insights into the principles of courage, divine timing, and the impact of individual actions.

2.3 Martin Luther King Jr.: A Modern-Day Prophet

Martin Luther King Jr. stands as a towering figure in modern history, whose life and work exemplify the power of recognizing and acting upon one's potential. Drawing deep inspiration from biblical principles, King led the civil rights movement in the United States, striving to end racial segregation and discrimination. His unwavering belief in justice, equality, and the potential for societal transformation drove his tireless efforts. This chapter explores King's life, his biblical inspiration, and his prophetic role in modern society, supported by comprehensive biblical teachings and references from Strong's Concordance.

2.3.1 Early Life and Call to Ministry

Martin Luther King Jr. was born on January 15, 1929, into a deeply religious family. His father and grandfather were Baptist ministers, and King followed in their footsteps, becoming a pastor at Dexter Avenue Baptist Church in Montgomery, Alabama. His spiritual upbringing and academic pursuits equipped him with a profound understanding of biblical teachings and social ethics.

2.3.2 Biblical Inspiration for Social Justice

King's commitment to social justice was deeply rooted in the Bible. One of his favorite scriptures was Amos 5:24 (NIV): "But let justice roll on like a river, righteousness like a never-failing stream!" The Hebrew word for justice, mishpat (H4941), signifies God's demand for fairness and equity in human affairs. King often cited this verse, emphasizing that true justice is continuous and transformative.

2.3.3 The Power of Love and Nonviolence

King's philosophy of nonviolence was inspired by Jesus' teachings in the Sermon on the Mount. Matthew 5:44 (NIV) states, "But I tell you, love your enemies and pray for those who persecute you." The Greek word for love used here is agapao (G25), denoting unconditional, selfless love. King believed that love and nonviolence were the most powerful tools for social change, a principle he articulated in his famous speech, "Loving Your Enemies."

2.3.4 The Prophetic Vision of Equality

King's vision for equality was deeply influenced by the prophetic tradition in the Old Testament. Isaiah 1:17 (NIV) exhorts, "Learn to do right; seek justice. Defend the oppressed. Take up the cause of the fatherless; plead the case of the widow." The term tsedeq (H6664), translated as righteousness or justice, underscores the moral imperative to advocate for the marginalized and oppressed.

2.3.5 Leadership in the Civil Rights Movement

King's leadership in the civil rights movement was marked by significant events such as the Montgomery Bus Boycott, the March on Washington, and the Selma to Montgomery marches. His ability to mobilize people and articulate a vision for a just society drew parallels to the biblical prophets who called nations to righteousness.

2.3.6 The "I Have a Dream" Speech

King's "I Have a Dream" speech, delivered during the March on Washington for Jobs and Freedom on August 28, 1963, is a prophetic declaration of hope and equality. He famously stated, "I have a dream that one day this nation will rise up and live out the true meaning of its creed: 'We hold these truths to be self-evident, that all men are created equal.'" This echoes the biblical principle found in Genesis 1:27

(NIV): "So God created mankind in his own image, in the image of God he created them; male and female he created them." The concept of Imago Dei (image of God) affirms the intrinsic worth and equality of every human being.

2.3.7 The Cost of Discipleship

King's commitment to his prophetic calling came at great personal cost. He faced constant threats, imprisonment, and ultimately assassination on April 4, 1968. His willingness to sacrifice his life for the cause of justice parallels the biblical concept of discipleship. Luke 9:23-24 (NIV) states, "Then he said to them all: 'Whoever wants to be my disciple must deny themselves and take up their cross daily and follow me. For whoever wants to save their life will lose it, but whoever loses their life for me will save it.'" King embodied this sacrificial commitment, demonstrating the ultimate expression of love and service.

Comprehensive Commentary

Amos 5:24: The Hebrew term mishpat (H4941) for justice is central to the prophetic call for social equity. This verse underscores the need for justice to be an ongoing, transformative process, aligning with King's vision for continuous social reform.

Matthew 5:44: The Greek term agapao (G25) for love reflects the selfless, unconditional nature of Christ's command to love one's enemies. King's adherence to nonviolence and love as powerful forces for change is deeply rooted in this teaching.

Isaiah 1:17: The call to "seek justice" (darash mishpat, H1875 and H4941) and "defend the oppressed" (ashar chamots, H833 and H2541) highlights the prophetic mandate to advocate for the marginalized. King's ministry exemplified this commitment to social justice.

Genesis 1:27: The concept of Imago Dei (image of God) asserts the inherent dignity and equality of all people. King's dream of a society where individuals are judged by the content of their character, not the color of their skin, is a direct reflection of this biblical truth.

Luke 9:23-24: The call to take up one's cross and follow Christ underscores the cost of discipleship. King's life and ultimate sacrifice resonate with this profound commitment to follow the path of righteousness, even unto death.

2.3.8 Lessons from Martin Luther King Jr.'s Life

King's life offers several key lessons for realizing our potential:

1. Courage in the Face of Injustice: King's unwavering stand against racial injustice exemplifies the courage needed to address systemic wrongs.

2. Power of Love and Nonviolence: His commitment to love and nonviolence as tools for social change reflects the transformative power of these principles.

3. Vision of Equality: King's prophetic vision for equality and justice is a reminder of the biblical mandate to advocate for the oppressed.

4. Sacrificial Leadership: His willingness to suffer and ultimately give his life for the cause of justice demonstrates the cost of true discipleship.

2.3.9 Relevance for Today

Martin Luther King Jr.'s legacy remains profoundly relevant for contemporary believers. It teaches that:

- Faith and Action: True faith must be accompanied by action. King's life exemplifies how faith can drive meaningful social change.

- Justice and Equality: The pursuit of justice and equality is a biblical imperative, calling us to advocate for the marginalized and oppressed.

- Hope and Perseverance: Despite significant challenges, King's dream for a better world inspires hope and perseverance in the ongoing struggle for justice.

Martin Luther King Jr. was a modern-day prophet whose life and work were deeply inspired by biblical principles. His commitment to justice, equality, and nonviolence transformed the landscape of American society and continues to inspire global movements for social justice. By exploring King's life through comprehensive biblical teachings and references from Strong's Concordance, we gain deeper insights into the principles of courage, love, and sacrifice that are essential for realizing our potential and advancing God's kingdom on earth.

CHAPTER 03

UNLOCKING YOUR POTENTIAL

3.1 Self-Discovery and Reflection

Unlocking one's potential begins with the journey of self-discovery and reflection. This process involves understanding our unique qualities, strengths, and the divine purpose embedded within us. Biblical teachings offer profound insights into the nature of self-discovery, emphasizing the importance of recognizing our inherent worth and capabilities as creations of God. This chapter explores the theological foundations and practical steps for self-discovery and reflection, supported by comprehensive biblical teachings and references from Strong's Concordance.

3.1.1 Theological Foundation of Self-Discovery

The journey of self-discovery is deeply rooted in the biblical understanding of human nature and divine creation. Psalm 139:14 (NIV) declares, "I praise you because I am fearfully and wonderfully made; your works are wonderful, I know that full well." The Hebrew term for "fearfully" (yare, H3372) conveys a sense of reverence and awe, while "wonderfully" (palah, H6381) signifies being set apart or distinguished. This verse emphasizes that each individual is uniquely crafted by God, possessing inherent value and purpose.

3.1.2 Recognizing Our Unique Qualities and Strengths

Recognizing our unique qualities and strengths is essential for unlocking our potential. Ephesians 2:10 (NIV) states, "For we are God's handiwork, created in Christ Jesus to do good works, which God prepared in advance for us to do." The term "handiwork" (poiema, G4161) implies a work of art or craftsmanship. This suggests that each person is a unique creation, designed by God with specific gifts and abilities.

3.1.3 The Role of Self-Reflection in Spiritual Growth

Self-reflection is a critical component of spiritual growth and self-discovery. 2 Corinthians 13:5 (NIV) urges,

"Examine yourselves to see whether you are in the faith; test yourselves. Do you not realize that Christ Jesus is in you—unless, of course, you fail the test?" The Greek term for "examine" (peirazo, G3985) means to test or scrutinize. This self-examination helps us to align our lives with God's will and identify areas for growth.

3.1.4 The Mirror of God's Word

James 1:23-24 (NIV) compares self-reflection to looking in a mirror: "Anyone who listens to the word but does not do what it says is like someone who looks at his face in a mirror and, after looking at himself, goes away and immediately forgets what he looks like." The term "mirror" (esoptron, G2072) symbolizes the word of God, which reflects our true nature and guides us in the process of self-discovery. Engaging with scripture allows us to see ourselves as God sees us, revealing both our strengths and areas needing transformation.

3.1.5 Embracing Our Identity in Christ

Understanding our identity in Christ is foundational for self-discovery. Galatians 2:20 (NIV) states, "I have been crucified with Christ and I no longer live, but Christ lives in me. The life I now live in the body, I live by faith in the Son of God, who loved me and gave himself for me." The phrase "Christ lives in me" (Christos en emoi, G5547 and G1698) signifies the indwelling presence of Christ, transforming our identity and purpose. Recognizing this truth empowers us to embrace our God-given potential.

Comprehensive Commentary

Psalm 139:14: The terms yare (H3372) and palah (H6381) highlight the awe-inspiring and distinct nature of God's creation. This verse calls us to recognize the divine craftsmanship in our being, fostering a sense of worth and purpose.

Ephesians 2:10: The term poiema (G4161) underscores the concept of being God's masterpiece. This passage encourages believers to appreciate their unique design and to seek out the good works God has prepared for them.

2 Corinthians 13:5: The Greek term peirazo (G3985) emphasizes the importance of self-examination in the faith journey. This self-reflection aligns us with God's standards and helps us to grow spiritually.

James 1:23-24: The term esoptron (G2072) illustrates the reflective nature of God's word. Engaging with scripture is essential for self-discovery, as it reveals our true selves and guides us toward spiritual maturity.

Galatians 2:20: The phrase Christos en emoi (G5547 and G1698) signifies the transformative presence of Christ within believers. This new identity in Christ is foundational for understanding and unlocking our potential.

3.1.6 Practical Steps for Self-Discovery and Reflection

1. Engage with Scripture: Regularly read and meditate on the Bible, allowing it to reveal your true identity and potential. Psalm 119:105 (NIV) states, "Your word is a lamp for my feet, a light on my path." The term "lamp" (ner, H5216) signifies guidance, illuminating the path to self-discovery.

2. Prayer and Meditation: Spend time in prayer and meditation, seeking God's guidance and clarity about your purpose. Philippians 4:6-7 (NIV) encourages, "Do not be anxious about anything, but in every situation, by prayer and petition, with thanksgiving, present your requests to God. And the peace of God, which transcends all understanding, will guard your hearts and your minds in Christ Jesus."

3. Journaling: Keep a journal to document your thoughts, reflections, and insights gained during your journey of self-discovery. This practice helps to clarify your thoughts and track your growth.

4. Seek Feedback: Engage with trusted friends, mentors, or spiritual leaders who can provide feedback and insights about your strengths and areas for growth. Proverbs 27:17 (NIV) states, "As iron sharpens iron, so one person sharpens another."

5. Embrace Silence and Solitude: Create moments of silence and solitude to reflect deeply on your life and purpose. Mark 1:35 (NIV) records Jesus' practice: "Very early in the morning, while it was still dark, Jesus got up, left the house and went off to a solitary place, where he prayed."

3.1.7 The Benefits of Self-Discovery and Reflection

- Increased Self-Awareness: Understanding your strengths, weaknesses, and unique qualities enhances self-awareness, enabling you to make informed decisions and pursue your potential effectively.

- Alignment with God's Will: Self-discovery aligns your life with God's purpose, fostering a deeper relationship with Him and guiding you towards fulfilling your divine calling.

- Enhanced Relationships: Recognizing and embracing your identity in Christ improves your relationships, as you interact with others from a place of authenticity and confidence.

- Personal Growth and Development: The process of self-reflection promotes continuous personal growth, equipping you to handle life's challenges and opportunities with resilience and wisdom.

3.1.8 Relevance for Today

The practice of self-discovery and reflection remains vital for contemporary believers. It teaches that:

- Intentional Living: By understanding and embracing our God-given identity and potential, we can live intentionally and purposefully.

- Spiritual Growth: Regular self-reflection fosters spiritual growth, drawing us closer to God and aligning our lives with His will.

- Empowerment: Recognizing our unique qualities and strengths empowers us to contribute meaningfully to our communities and the broader world.

Self-discovery and reflection are foundational steps in unlocking our potential. By engaging with scripture, prayer, and intentional reflection, we can recognize our unique qualities and strengths, align our lives with God's purpose, and embrace our identity in Christ. This journey not only enhances our self-awareness and personal growth but also empowers us to fulfill our divine calling. Through comprehensive biblical teachings and references from Strong's Concordance, we gain deeper insights into the importance and process of self-discovery and reflection.

3.1 Self-Discovery and Reflection

Unlocking one's potential begins with the journey of self-discovery and reflection. This process involves understanding our unique qualities, strengths, and the divine purpose embedded within us. Biblical teachings offer profound insights into the nature of self-discovery, emphasizing the importance of recognizing our inherent worth and capabilities as creations of God. This chapter explores the theological foundations and practical steps for self-discovery and reflection, supported by comprehensive biblical teachings and references from Strong's Concordance.

3.1.1 Theological Foundation of Self-Discovery

The journey of self-discovery is deeply rooted in the biblical understanding of human nature and divine creation. Psalm 139:14 (NIV) declares, "I praise you because I am fearfully and wonderfully made; your works are wonderful, I know that full well." The Hebrew term for "fearfully" (yare, H3372) conveys a sense of reverence and awe, while "wonderfully" (palah, H6381) signifies being set apart or distinguished. This verse emphasizes that each individual is uniquely crafted by God, possessing inherent value and purpose.

3.1.2 Recognizing Our Unique Qualities and Strengths

Recognizing our unique qualities and strengths is essential for unlocking our potential. Ephesians 2:10 (NIV) states, "For we are God's handiwork, created in Christ Jesus to do good works, which God prepared in advance for us to do." The term "handiwork" (poiema, G4161) implies a work of art or craftsmanship. This suggests that each person is a unique creation, designed by God with specific gifts and abilities.

3.1.3 The Role of Self-Reflection in Spiritual Growth

Self-reflection is a critical component of spiritual growth and self-discovery. 2 Corinthians 13:5 (NIV) urges, "Examine yourselves to see whether you are in the faith; test yourselves. Do you not realize that Christ Jesus is in you—unless, of course, you fail the test?" The Greek term for "examine" (peirazo, G3985) means to test or scrutinize. This self-examination helps us to align our lives with God's will and identify areas for growth.

3.1.4 The Mirror of God's Word

James 1:23-24 (NIV) compares self-reflection to looking in a mirror: "Anyone who listens to the word but does not do what it says is like someone who looks at his face in a mirror and, after looking at himself, goes away and immediately forgets what he looks like." The term "mirror" (esoptron, G2072) symbolizes the word of God, which reflects our true nature and guides us in the process of self-discovery. Engaging with scripture allows us to see ourselves as God sees us, revealing both our strengths and areas needing transformation.

3.1.5 Embracing Our Identity in Christ

Understanding our identity in Christ is foundational for self-discovery. Galatians 2:20 (NIV) states, "I have been crucified with Christ and I no longer live, but Christ lives in me. The life I now live in the body, I live by faith in the Son of God, who loved me and gave himself for me." The phrase "Christ lives in me" (Christos en emoi, G5547 and G1698) signifies the indwelling presence of Christ, transforming our identity and purpose. Recognizing this truth empowers us to embrace our God-given potential.

Comprehensive Commentary

Psalm 139:14: The terms yare (H3372) and palah (H6381) highlight the awe-inspiring and distinct nature of God's creation. This verse calls us to recognize the divine craftsmanship in our being, fostering a sense of worth and purpose.

Ephesians 2:10: The term poiema (G4161) underscores the concept of being God's masterpiece. This passage encourages believers to appreciate their unique design and to seek out the good works God has prepared for them.

2 Corinthians 13:5: The Greek term peirazo (G3985) emphasizes the importance of self-examination in the faith journey. This self-reflection aligns us with God's standards and helps us to grow spiritually.

James 1:23-24: The term esoptron (G2072) illustrates the reflective nature of God's word. Engaging with scripture is essential for self-discovery, as it reveals our true selves and guides us toward spiritual maturity.

Galatians 2:20: The phrase Christos en emoi (G5547 and G1698) signifies the transformative presence of Christ within believers. This new identity in Christ is foundational for understanding and unlocking our potential.

3.1.6 Practical Steps for Self-Discovery and Reflection

1. Engage with Scripture: Regularly read and meditate on the Bible, allowing it to reveal your true identity and potential. Psalm 119:105 (NIV) states, "Your word is a lamp for my feet, a light on my path." The term "lamp" (ner, H5216) signifies guidance, illuminating the path to self-discovery.

2. Prayer and Meditation: Spend time in prayer and meditation, seeking God's guidance and clarity about your purpose. Philippians 4:6-7 (NIV) encourages, "Do not be anxious about anything, but in every situation, by prayer and petition, with thanksgiving, present your requests to God. And the peace of God, which transcends all understanding, will guard your hearts and your minds in Christ Jesus."

3. Journaling: Keep a journal to document your thoughts, reflections, and insights gained during your journey of self-discovery. This practice helps to clarify your thoughts and track your growth.

4. Seek Feedback: Engage with trusted friends, mentors, or spiritual leaders who can provide feedback and insights about your strengths and areas for growth. Proverbs 27:17 (NIV) states, "As iron sharpens iron, so one person sharpens another."

5. Embrace Silence and Solitude: Create moments of silence and solitude to reflect deeply on your life and purpose. Mark 1:35 (NIV) records Jesus' practice: "Very early in the morning, while it was still dark, Jesus got up, left the house and went off to a solitary place, where he prayed."

3.1.7 The Benefits of Self-Discovery and Reflection

- Increased Self-Awareness: Understanding your strengths, weaknesses, and unique qualities enhances self-awareness, enabling you to make informed decisions and pursue your potential effectively.

- Alignment with God's Will: Self-discovery aligns your life with God's purpose, fostering a deeper relationship with Him and guiding you towards fulfilling your divine calling.

- Enhanced Relationships: Recognizing and embracing your identity in Christ improves your relationships, as you interact with others from a place of authenticity and confidence.

- Personal Growth and Development: The process of self-reflection promotes continuous personal growth, equipping you to handle life's challenges and opportunities with resilience and wisdom.

3.1.8 Relevance for Today

The practice of self-discovery and reflection remains vital for contemporary believers. It teaches that:

- Intentional Living: By understanding and embracing our God-given identity and potential, we can live intentionally and purposefully.

- Spiritual Growth: Regular self-reflection fosters spiritual growth, drawing us closer to God and aligning our lives with His will.

- Empowerment: Recognizing our unique qualities and strengths empowers us to contribute meaningfully to our communities and the broader world.

Self-discovery and reflection are foundational steps in unlocking our potential. By engaging with scripture, prayer, and intentional reflection, we can recognize our unique qualities and strengths, align our lives with God's purpose, and embrace our identity in Christ. This journey not only enhances our self-awareness and personal growth but also empowers us to fulfill our divine calling. Through comprehensive biblical teachings and references from Strong's Concordance, we gain deeper insights into the importance and process of self-discovery and reflection.

3.2 Seeking God's Guidance

Seeking God's guidance is crucial for unlocking our potential and fulfilling our divine purpose. Proverbs 3:5-6 (NIV) states, "Trust in the Lord with all your heart and lean not on your own understanding; in all your ways submit to him, and he will make your paths straight." This chapter explores the importance of seeking God's guidance, practical ways to do so, and the biblical foundation supporting this practice. It also includes comprehensive commentary with references from Strong's Concordance.

3.2.1 Trusting in the Lord

The foundation of seeking God's guidance begins with trust. Proverbs 3:5 (NIV) instructs us to "Trust in the Lord with all your heart." The Hebrew word for trust, batach (H982), means to have confidence, be bold, and secure. Trusting in God requires a complete reliance on Him, acknowledging His sovereignty and wisdom.

3.2.2 Lean Not on Your Own Understanding

Proverbs 3:5 continues, "lean not on your own understanding." The Hebrew word for lean, sha'an (H8172), implies support or reliance. This verse advises us to not depend solely on our limited human perspective but to seek divine insight. Jeremiah 17:9 (NIV) reminds us, "The heart is deceitful above all things and beyond cure. Who can understand it?" This underscores the necessity of relying on God's wisdom over our own.

3.2.3 Submitting to God in All Ways

Proverbs 3:6 (NIV) states, "in all your ways submit to him, and he will make your paths straight." The Hebrew word for submit, yada (H3045), means to know, acknowledge, or recognize. This implies a conscious and deliberate effort to recognize God's authority in every aspect of our lives. Submission to God aligns our actions with His will, ensuring we follow the right path.

3.2.4 The Role of Prayer and Meditation

Seeking God's guidance is deeply intertwined with prayer and meditation. Philippians 4:6-7 (NIV) advises, "Do not be anxious about anything, but in every situation, by prayer and petition, with thanksgiving, present your requests to God. And the peace of God, which transcends all understanding, will guard your hearts and your minds in Christ Jesus." The Greek term for prayer, proseuche (G4335), denotes earnest and directed communication with God. Through prayer, we seek God's will and direction.

3.2.5 The Importance of Scripture

God's word is a primary source of guidance. Psalm 119:105 (NIV) declares, "Your word is a lamp for my feet, a light on my path." The Hebrew word for lamp, ner (H5216), signifies illumination and direction. Engaging with scripture provides clarity and insight into God's will, guiding us in making decisions aligned with His purpose.

3.2.6 Seeking Counsel from Wise Advisors

Proverbs 15:22 (NIV) states, "Plans fail for lack of counsel, but with many advisers they succeed." The Hebrew term for counsel, tachbulah (H8458), refers to advice or guidance. Seeking counsel from godly and wise advisors helps us gain different perspectives and discern God's direction more clearly.

3.2.7 Waiting on the Lord

Isaiah 40:31 (NIV) encourages, "but those who hope in the Lord will renew their strength. They will soar on wings like eagles; they will run and not grow weary, they will walk and not be faint." The Hebrew word for hope, qavah (H6960), means to wait with expectation. Patience and waiting on God's timing are essential aspects of seeking His guidance.

Comprehensive Commentary

Proverbs 3:5-6: The terms batach (H982) and sha'an (H8172) emphasize the need for complete reliance on God over our understanding. Yada (H3045) highlights the importance of acknowledging God in every aspect of our lives to align with His will.

Jeremiah 17:9: The verse underscores human limitations, highlighting the necessity of divine wisdom over our understanding.

Philippians 4:6-7: The Greek term proseuche (G4335) for prayer signifies an earnest seeking of God's will, coupled with the peace that follows, which surpasses human understanding.

Psalm 119:105: The term ner (H5216) illustrates the guiding role of scripture in our lives, providing illumination and direction.

Proverbs 15:22: The term tachbulah (H8458) emphasizes the value of seeking wise counsel to ensure success in our plans.

Isaiah 40:31: The term qavah (H6960) reflects the importance of waiting with expectation, relying on God's timing for strength and guidance.

3.2.8 Practical Steps for Seeking God's Guidance

1. Daily Prayer: Make prayer a daily practice, seeking God's direction in all decisions. Jesus modeled this in Mark 1:35 (NIV): "Very early in the morning, while it was still dark, Jesus got up, left the house and went off to a solitary place, where he prayed."

2. Meditate on Scripture: Spend time reading and meditating on the Bible. Joshua 1:8 (NIV) advises, "Keep this

Book of the Law always on your lips; meditate on it day and night, so that you may be careful to do everything written in it. Then you will be prosperous and successful."

3. Seek Wise Counsel: Consult with trusted spiritual mentors and advisors who can offer godly wisdom. Proverbs 11:14 (NIV) states, "For lack of guidance a nation falls, but victory is won through many advisers."

4. Wait on God: Practice patience and trust in God's timing. Psalm 27:14 (NIV) encourages, "Wait for the Lord; be strong and take heart and wait for the Lord."

5. Journal Your Journey: Write down your prayers, insights, and the ways you sense God's guidance. This helps in reflecting on His faithfulness and direction over time.

3.2.9 The Benefits of Seeking God's Guidance

- Clarity and Direction: Seeking God's guidance provides clarity and direction in our decisions, helping us avoid confusion and missteps.

- Peace and Assurance: Trusting in God brings peace, knowing that He is in control and will lead us on the right path.

- Alignment with God's Will: Regularly seeking God's guidance ensures that our actions and decisions align with His divine purpose.

- Strength and Confidence: Depending on God's guidance empowers us with strength and confidence to face challenges and pursue our potential.

3.2.10 Relevance for Today

Seeking God's guidance remains vital for contemporary believers. It teaches that:

Dependence on God: True potential is realized through dependence on God rather than self-reliance.

- Spiritual Discipline: Consistent prayer, meditation, and seeking counsel are essential spiritual disciplines.

- Trust in God's Sovereignty: Trusting in God's timing and wisdom brings peace and assurance in navigating life's complexities.

Seeking God's guidance is essential for unlocking our potential and fulfilling our divine purpose. By trusting in God, engaging in prayer and meditation, consulting wise advisors, and waiting on His timing, we align our lives with His will. This journey not only brings clarity, direction, and peace but also empowers us to walk confidently in our God-given path. Through comprehensive biblical teachings and references from Strong's Concordance, we gain deeper insights into the importance and practice of seeking God's guidance.

3.3 Overcoming Obstacles

Overcoming obstacles is an essential part of realizing our potential. Life is filled with challenges that can hinder our progress and test our resolve. However, with God's strength and perseverance, we can overcome these obstacles and continue moving forward. Philippians 4:13 (NIV) declares, "I can do all this through him who gives me strength." This chapter explores the biblical principles of overcoming obstacles, practical steps for facing challenges, and the theological foundations that support this journey, using comprehensive commentary and references from Strong's Concordance.

3.3.1 The Promise of Strength

Philippians 4:13 (NIV) provides a powerful promise: "I can do all this through him who gives me strength." The Greek word for strength, endunamoo (G1743), means to empower or enable. This verse assures us that our strength comes from Christ, empowering us to face and overcome obstacles.

3.3.2 The Role of Faith in Overcoming Obstacles

Faith is a critical component in overcoming challenges. Hebrews 11:1 (NIV) defines faith as "confidence in what we hope for and assurance about what we do not see." The Greek word for faith, pistis (G4102), signifies trust and belief. Faith enables us to see beyond our current difficulties and trust in God's promises.

3.3.3 Biblical Examples of Overcoming Obstacles

David and Goliath: David's victory over Goliath is a classic example of overcoming seemingly insurmountable obstacles. 1 Samuel 17:45-47 (NIV) records David's faith and reliance on God: "David said to the Philistine, 'You come against me with sword and spear and javelin, but I come against you in the name of the Lord Almighty, the God of the armies of Israel, whom you have defied... All those gathered here will know that it is not by sword or spear that the Lord saves; for the battle is the Lord's, and he will give all of you into our hands.'" David's confidence was in God's power, not his own.

Moses and the Red Sea: When faced with the Red Sea and the pursuing Egyptian army, Moses demonstrated faith in God's deliverance. Exodus 14:13-14 (NIV) states, "Moses answered the people, 'Do not be afraid. Stand firm and you will see the deliverance the Lord will bring you today... The Lord will fight for you; you need only to be still.'" The parting of the Red Sea illustrates God's power to make a way through impossible situations.

Paul's Perseverance: The Apostle Paul faced numerous obstacles, including imprisonment, beatings, and shipwrecks. In 2 Corinthians 12:9-10 (NIV), Paul writes, "But he said to me, 'My grace is sufficient for you, for my power is made perfect in weakness.' Therefore I will boast all the more gladly about my weaknesses, so that Christ's power may rest on me... For when I am weak, then I am strong." Paul's reliance on God's grace enabled him to persevere through hardships.

3.3.4 Practical Steps for Overcoming Obstacles

1. Rely on God's Strength: Acknowledge that your strength comes from God. Isaiah 40:31 (NIV) states, "But those who hope in the Lord will renew their strength. They will soar on wings like eagles; they will run and not grow weary, they will walk and not be faint." The Hebrew word for hope, qavah (H6960), signifies waiting with expectation.

2. Maintain a Positive Attitude: Focus on God's promises and maintain a positive attitude. Romans 8:28 (NIV) assures, "And we know that in all things God works for the good of those who love him, who have been called according to his purpose."

3. Pray for Guidance and Strength: Regularly seek God's guidance and strength through prayer. James 1:5 (NIV) encourages, "If any of you lacks wisdom, you should ask God, who gives generously to all without finding fault, and it will be given to you."

4. Stay Persistent: Do not give up when faced with challenges. Galatians 6:9 (NIV) states, "Let us not become

weary in doing good, for at the proper time we will reap a harvest if we do not give up."

5. Seek Support from Others: Surround yourself with supportive and godly people who can encourage you. Ecclesiastes 4:9-10 (NIV) says, "Two are better than one, because they have a good return for their labor: If either of them falls down, one can help the other up."

3.3.5 Theological Foundations of Overcoming Obstacles

God's Sovereignty and Power: God's sovereignty assures us that He is in control, even in the midst of challenges. Psalm 46:1 (NIV) declares, "God is our refuge and strength, an ever-present help in trouble."

The Presence of the Holy Spirit: The Holy Spirit empowers us to overcome obstacles. Acts 1:8 (NIV) states, "But you will receive power when the Holy Spirit comes on you; and you will be my witnesses in Jerusalem, and in all Judea and Samaria, and to the ends of the earth." The Greek word for power, dynamis (G1411), denotes miraculous power and strength.

The Promise of Victory: The Bible assures us of victory through Christ. 1 Corinthians 15:57 (NIV) proclaims, "But thanks be to God! He gives us the victory through our Lord Jesus Christ."

Comprehensive Commentary

Philippians 4:13: The term endunamoo (G1743) emphasizes that our strength and ability to overcome obstacles come from Christ's empowerment.

Hebrews 11:1: The term pistis (G4102) signifies trust and belief, highlighting the importance of faith in overcoming challenges.

1 Samuel 17:45-47: David's reliance on God's power (yad, H3027) rather than human strength illustrates the principle of divine empowerment.

Exodus 14:13-14: Moses' assurance of God's deliverance (yeshua, H3444) underscores the theme of divine intervention in overcoming obstacles.

2 Corinthians 12:9-10: Paul's acceptance of weakness (astheneia, G769) as a platform for Christ's power (dynamis, G1411) highlights the paradox of strength in weakness.

Isaiah 40:31: The term qavah (H6960) reflects waiting with expectation, emphasizing reliance on God's timing and strength.

Romans 8:28: The assurance of God working for good (agathos, G18) provides a foundation for maintaining a positive outlook amidst challenges.

James 1:5: The promise of wisdom (sophia, G4678) from God highlights the importance of seeking divine guidance in overcoming obstacles.

Galatians 6:9: The encouragement to not give up (ekkakeo, G1573) underscores the importance of persistence in the face of challenges.

Ecclesiastes 4:9-10: The benefits of companionship (chaber, H2267) emphasize the importance of support from others in overcoming difficulties.

Psalm 46:1: The declaration of God as our refuge (machaseh, H4268) and strength (oz, H5797) reinforces the theological foundation of divine support in overcoming obstacles.

Acts 1:8: The term dynamis (G1411) underscores the empowering presence of the Holy Spirit, enabling believers to overcome challenges.

1 Corinthians 15:57: The assurance of victory (nikos, G3534) through Christ provides a foundation for confidence in overcoming obstacles.

3.3.6 Relevance for Today

The practice of overcoming obstacles remains vital for contemporary believers. It teaches that:

- Dependence on God's Strength: True potential is realized through dependence on God's strength rather than self-reliance.

- Faith and Perseverance: Faith in God's promises and perseverance in the face of challenges are essential for overcoming obstacles.

- Community Support: The support and encouragement of a faith community are invaluable in navigating difficulties.

Overcoming obstacles is an integral part of unlocking our potential. By relying on God's strength, maintaining faith, seeking guidance through prayer, and surrounding ourselves with supportive individuals, we can face and overcome challenges. This journey not only strengthens our character but also aligns us with God's purpose and empowers us to fulfill our divine calling. Through comprehensive biblical teachings and references from Strong's Concordance, we gain deeper insights into the principles and practices of overcoming obstacles.

CHAPTER 04

CULTIVATING POTENITAL IN OTHERS

4.1 Mentorship and Encouragement

Mentorship and encouragement are powerful tools in helping others realize their potential. The relationship between Paul and Timothy in the New Testament provides a clear biblical example of how effective mentorship can nurture and develop one's abilities and character. This chapter explores the importance of mentorship and encouragement, drawing on biblical teachings and expository commentary with comprehensive references from Strong's Concordance.

4.1.1 The Biblical Basis for Mentorship

Paul's relationship with Timothy is a model of effective mentorship. 1 Timothy 4:12 (NIV) states, "Don't let anyone look down on you because you are young, but set an example for the believers in speech, in conduct, in love, in faith and in purity." The Greek word for example, typos (G5179), means a model or pattern to be followed. Paul's advice to Timothy highlights the importance of being a role model and encouraging others to do the same.

4.1.2 Characteristics of a Good Mentor

A good mentor exhibits several key characteristics, as demonstrated by Paul:

- Wisdom and Experience: Paul's letters to Timothy are filled with practical advice and theological insights, showing his deep understanding and experience. James 3:13 (NIV) says, "Who is wise and understanding among you? Let them show it by their good life, by deeds done in the humility that comes from wisdom." The Greek word for wisdom, sophia (G4678), denotes not just knowledge but the application of knowledge in practical ways.

- Encouragement: Paul consistently encouraged Timothy, recognizing the importance of building him up. 1 Thessalonians 5:11 (NIV) states, "Therefore encourage one another and build each other up, just as in fact you are doing." The Greek word for encourage, parakaleo (G3870), means to call to one's side, to comfort, and to exhort.

- Patience and Understanding: Effective mentorship requires patience and a deep understanding of the mentee's strengths and weaknesses. 2 Timothy 2:24 (NIV) says, "And the Lord's servant must not be quarrelsome but must be kind to everyone, able to teach, not resentful." The term makrothumeo (G3114) signifies patience and long-suffering.

4.1.3 The Impact of Encouragement

Encouragement plays a crucial role in helping others realize their potential. Hebrews 10:24-25 (NIV) encourages believers to, "consider how we may spur one another on toward love and good deeds, not giving up meeting together, as some are in the habit of doing, but encouraging one another—and all the more as you see the Day approaching." The Greek word for spur, paroxysmos (G3948), means to provoke or stimulate.

4.1.4 Practical Ways to Mentor and Encourage Others

1. Be a Role Model: Demonstrate integrity, faith, and love in your actions. 1 Corinthians 11:1 (NIV) states, "Follow my example, as I follow the example of Christ." The Greek word for example, mimetes (G3402), means an imitator.

2. Provide Guidance and Advice: Share your wisdom and experiences to help guide others. Proverbs 11:14 (NIV) states, "For lack of guidance a nation falls, but victory is won

through many advisers." The Hebrew word for guidance, tachbulah (H8458), implies counsel and direction.

3. Encourage and Uplift: Offer words of encouragement and support. Colossians 4:6 (NIV) says, "Let your conversation be always full of grace, seasoned with salt, so that you may know how to answer everyone." The Greek word for grace, charis (G5485), denotes kindness and favor.

4. Be Patient and Understanding: Recognize that growth takes time and be patient with the process. Galatians 6:9 (NIV) encourages, "Let us not become weary in doing good, for at the proper time we will reap a harvest if we do not give up."

5. Pray for Your Mentees: Regularly pray for those you are mentoring. James 5:16 (NIV) states, "Therefore confess your sins to each other and pray for each other so that you may be healed. The prayer of a righteous person is powerful and effective." The Greek word for prayer, euche (G2171), emphasizes earnest and fervent supplication.

4.1.5 Biblical Examples of Mentorship and Encouragement

Moses and Joshua: Moses mentored Joshua, preparing him to lead the Israelites. Deuteronomy 31:7-8 (NIV) records Moses' encouragement: "Then Moses summoned Joshua and said to him in the presence of all Israel, 'Be strong and courageous, for you must go with this people into the land that the Lord swore to their ancestors to give them, and you must divide it among them as their inheritance. The Lord himself goes before you and will be with you; he will never leave you nor forsake you. Do not be afraid; do not be discouraged.'"

Elijah and Elisha: Elijah mentored Elisha, passing on his prophetic mantle. 2 Kings 2:9 (NIV) states, "When they had crossed, Elijah said to Elisha, 'Tell me, what can I do for you before I am taken from you?' 'Let me inherit a double portion of your spirit,' Elisha replied."

Paul and Timothy: Paul's mentorship of Timothy is evident throughout his letters, providing guidance, encouragement, and instruction. 2 Timothy 1:6-7 (NIV) states, "For this reason I remind you to fan into flame the gift of God, which is in you through the laying on of my hands. For the Spirit God gave us does not make us timid, but gives us power, love and self-discipline."

Comprehensive Commentary

1 Timothy 4:12: The term typos (G5179) highlights the importance of being a model or pattern for others. Paul encourages Timothy to set an example in speech (logos, G3056), conduct (anastrophe, G391), love (agape, G26), faith (pistis, G4102), and purity (hagneia, G47).

James 3:13: The term sophia (G4678) emphasizes the application of knowledge in practical and ethical ways, reflecting true wisdom.

1 Thessalonians 5:11: The term parakaleo (G3870) signifies calling to one's side for comfort, encouragement, and exhortation, highlighting the supportive role of a mentor.

2 Timothy 2:24: The term makrothumeo (G3114) signifies patience and long-suffering, essential qualities for a mentor.

Hebrews 10:24-25: The term paroxysmos (G3948) emphasizes the need to provoke or stimulate others towards love and good deeds, reflecting the role of encouragement.

1 Corinthians 11:1: The term mimetes (G3402) highlights the importance of being an imitator of Christ and a model for others.

Proverbs 11:14: The term tachbulah (H8458) underscores the importance of counsel and guidance in decision-making and leadership.

Colossians 4:6: The term charis (G5485) reflects kindness and favor in communication, essential for encouraging others.

James 5:16: The term euche (G2171) emphasizes earnest and fervent prayer, highlighting the importance of spiritual support in mentorship.

4.1.6 Relevance for Today

Mentorship and encouragement remain vital for contemporary believers. They teach that:

- Guiding the Next Generation: Mentorship helps nurture and develop the potential of future leaders.

- Building Strong Communities: Encouragement fosters a supportive and uplifting community, essential for spiritual growth.

- Reflecting Christ's Love: By mentoring and encouraging others, we reflect Christ's love and commitment to nurturing others.

Mentorship and encouragement are powerful tools in helping others realize their potential. By being a role model, providing guidance, offering encouragement, exercising patience, and praying for our mentees, we can significantly impact their growth and development. Through comprehensive biblical teachings and references from Strong's Concordance, we gain deeper insights into the principles and practices of effective mentorship and encouragement.

4.2 Building a Supportive Community

Building a supportive community is crucial for fostering growth and helping individuals unlock their potential. The Bible emphasizes the importance of community and mutual encouragement, while psychology and philosophy offer additional insights into the benefits of communal support. This chapter explores the biblical foundation for building a supportive community, supplemented with psychological and philosophical perspectives.

4.2.1 The Biblical Foundation for Community

The Bible consistently underscores the importance of community and mutual support. Hebrews 10:24-25 (NIV) states, "And let us consider how we may spur one another on toward love and good deeds, not giving up meeting together, as some are in the habit of doing, but encouraging one another—and all the more as you see the Day approaching." The Greek term for spur, paroxysmos (G3948), means to provoke or stimulate, indicating that community members should actively encourage one another towards positive actions.

4.2.2 The Role of Community in Spiritual Growth

The early church serves as a model for community life. Acts 2:42-47 (NIV) describes the fellowship of believers: "They devoted themselves to the apostles' teaching and to fellowship, to the breaking of bread and to prayer... All the believers were together and had everything in common. They sold property and possessions to give to anyone who had need... They broke bread in their homes and ate together with glad and sincere hearts, praising God and enjoying the favor of all the people." This passage highlights the elements of a supportive community: shared learning, mutual support, communal meals, and collective worship.

4.2.3 Encouragement and Accountability

Galatians 6:2 (NIV) encourages believers to "Carry each other's burdens, and in this way you will fulfill the law of Christ." The Greek word for burdens, baros (G922), signifies heavy loads, indicating that community members should support each other through difficult times. Additionally, Proverbs 27:17 (NIV) states, "As iron sharpens iron, so one person sharpens another," underscoring the role of accountability and mutual growth within a community.

4.2.4 Psychological Perspective on Community

Psychology recognizes the profound impact of community on mental health and personal development. Social support is linked to lower levels of stress, improved mental health, and increased resilience. According to the American Psychological Association, social support can buffer the effects of stress and provide individuals with a sense of belonging and security.

1. Sense of Belonging: Maslow's hierarchy of needs identifies belongingness as a fundamental human need. A

supportive community satisfies this need, providing individuals with a sense of acceptance and inclusion.

2. Emotional Support: Emotional support from community members can enhance self-esteem and reduce feelings of isolation. Studies show that individuals with strong social connections are less likely to experience depression and anxiety.

3. Instrumental Support: Practical assistance, such as help with tasks or financial support, can alleviate stress and enable individuals to focus on personal growth and development.

4.2.5 Philosophical Perspective on Community

Philosophers have long acknowledged the importance of community in human flourishing. Aristotle, in his work Nicomachean Ethics, posits that humans are inherently social beings and that community life is essential for achieving eudaimonia, or flourishing. He argues that friendships and communal relationships are vital for moral development and personal well-being.

1. Virtue and Community: Aristotle asserts that virtues are developed and exercised within the context of a community. Friendship and communal living provide opportunities for practicing virtues such as kindness, generosity, and justice.

2. Interdependence: The concept of interdependence suggests that individuals thrive when they rely on and contribute to the well-being of their community. This mutual dependence fosters a sense of purpose and belonging.

3. Common Good: Philosophers like John Stuart Mill and contemporary thinkers emphasize the importance of the common good. A supportive community works towards the common good, ensuring that the needs of all members are met and promoting collective well-being.

4.2.6 Practical Steps for Building a Supportive Community

1. Foster Open Communication: Encourage honest and open communication among community members. James 1:19 (NIV) advises, "Everyone should be quick to listen, slow to speak and slow to become angry."

2. Promote Mutual Respect and Understanding: Create an environment where differences are respected and valued. Romans 12:10 (NIV) states, "Be devoted to one another in love. Honor one another above yourselves."

3. Encourage Active Participation: Involve all members in community activities and decision-making processes. 1 Peter 4:10 (NIV) emphasizes, "Each of you should use whatever gift you have received to serve others, as faithful stewards of God's grace in its various forms."

4. Provide Support and Resources: Offer practical support and resources to those in need. Acts 4:34-35 (NIV) describes the early church's approach: "There were no needy persons among them. For from time to time those who owned land or houses sold them, brought the money from the sales and put it at the apostles' feet, and it was distributed to anyone who had need."

5. Cultivate a Culture of Encouragement: Regularly encourage and uplift one another. 1 Thessalonians 5:11 (NIV) states, "Therefore encourage one another and build each other up, just as in fact you are doing."

4.2.7 The Benefits of a Supportive Community

- Enhanced Personal Growth: A supportive community provides a nurturing environment for personal and spiritual growth.

- Increased Resilience: The support and encouragement from community members increase individuals' resilience to stress and adversity.

- Stronger Relationships: Building strong, supportive relationships enhances overall well-being and life satisfaction.

- Collective Impact: A united community can achieve more significant positive impacts than individuals working alone.

4.2.8 Relevance for Today

Building a supportive community is essential for contemporary believers. It teaches that:

- Mutual Support: Mutual support and encouragement are vital for personal and collective growth.

- Communal Responsibility: Every community member has a responsibility to contribute to the well-being of others.

- Spiritual and Emotional Health: A supportive community promotes both spiritual and emotional health, leading to a more fulfilled and resilient life.

Building a supportive community is crucial for fostering growth and helping individuals unlock their potential. By following biblical principles, incorporating psychological insights, and embracing philosophical perspectives, we can create environments that nurture and empower each member. Through comprehensive biblical teachings and practical steps, we gain deeper insights into the importance and practice of building a supportive community.

4.3 Theological Perspective on Building a Supportive Community

Theological perspectives on building a supportive community are rooted in the biblical narrative and teachings that emphasize the importance of communal life. From the creation of humanity to the formation of the early church, the Bible underscores the necessity of living in community. This chapter explores the theological foundations for building a supportive community, drawing insights from biblical examples, teachings, and principles that illustrate how a community can reflect God's love and foster spiritual growth.

4.3.1 The Nature of God and Community

The concept of community is inherent in the nature of God. The doctrine of the Trinity reveals that God exists in a perfect community of three Persons: Father, Son, and Holy Spirit. This divine community exemplifies perfect love, unity, and cooperation. Genesis 1:26 (NIV) states, "Then God said, 'Let us make mankind in our image, in our likeness.'" The use of "us" and "our" indicates the communal nature of God, and being made in His image means humans are designed for community.

4.3.2 Biblical Foundations for Community

The Bible provides numerous examples and teachings that emphasize the importance of community.

The Creation of Humanity: In Genesis 2:18 (NIV), God declares, "It is not good for the man to be alone. I will make a helper suitable for him." This highlights the inherent need for companionship and community.

The Covenant Community of Israel: God's covenant with Israel established a community bound by shared faith and mutual responsibility. Deuteronomy 6:4-5 (NIV) commands, "Hear, O Israel: The Lord our God, the Lord is one. Love the Lord your God with all your heart and with all your soul and with all your strength." The Shema emphasizes communal worship and devotion to God.

The Early Church: Acts 2:42-47 (NIV) describes the fellowship of believers: "They devoted themselves to the apostles' teaching and to fellowship, to the breaking of bread and to prayer... All the believers were together and had everything in common." This passage illustrates the early church's commitment to communal life, mutual support, and collective worship.

4.3.3 Theological Principles of Community

Several key theological principles underpin the concept of building a supportive community:

Love and Mutual Care: John 13:34-35 (NIV) records Jesus' command, "A new command I give you: Love one another. As I have loved you, so you must love one another. By this everyone will know that you are my disciples, if you love one another." The Greek word for love, agape (G26), denotes selfless, sacrificial love that seeks the best for others.

Unity in Diversity: 1 Corinthians 12:12-14 (NIV) states, "Just as a body, though one, has many parts, but all its many parts form one body, so it is with Christ... Now if the foot should say, 'Because I am not a hand, I do not belong to the body,' it would not for that reason stop being part of the body." This passage emphasizes the diversity of gifts within the body of Christ and the need for unity and mutual dependence.

Bearing One Another's Burdens: Galatians 6:2 (NIV) commands, "Carry each other's burdens, and in this way you will fulfill the law of Christ." The Greek word for burdens, baros (G922), signifies heavy loads that can overwhelm individuals. The community is called to provide support and relief.

Hospitality and Generosity: Hebrews 13:2 (NIV) advises, "Do not forget to show hospitality to strangers, for by so doing some people have shown hospitality to angels without knowing it." Hospitality (philoxenia, G5381) involves welcoming and caring for others, especially those in need.

Encouragement and Edification: 1 Thessalonians 5:11 (NIV) states, "Therefore encourage one another and build each other up, just as in fact you are doing." The Greek word for encourage, parakaleo (G3870), means to comfort, exhort, and strengthen. The community should be a source of encouragement and spiritual growth.

4.3.4 Practical Steps for Building a Supportive Community

1. Foster Genuine Relationships: Encourage authentic and deep relationships within the community. Romans 12:10 (NIV) states, "Be devoted to one another in love. Honor one another above yourselves." Genuine relationships are built on mutual respect and love.

2. Promote Inclusivity and Diversity: Embrace and celebrate the diversity within the community. Galatians 3:28 (NIV) declares, "There is neither Jew nor Gentile, neither slave nor free, nor is there male and female, for you are all one in Christ Jesus."

3. Encourage Participation and Service: Involve all members in the life of the community, encouraging them to use their gifts in service to others. 1 Peter 4:10 (NIV) states, "Each of you should use whatever gift you have received to serve others, as faithful stewards of God's grace in its various forms."

4. Provide Support and Care: Establish systems to support members in times of need, including prayer, counseling, and practical assistance. James 5:16 (NIV) says, "Therefore confess your sins to each other and pray for each other so that you may be healed. The prayer of a righteous person is powerful and effective."

5. Cultivate a Culture of Encouragement: Regularly offer words of encouragement and affirmation to build each

other up. Ephesians 4:29 (NIV) advises, "Do not let any unwholesome talk come out of your mouths, but only what is helpful for building others up according to their needs, that it may benefit those who listen."

4.3.5 The Benefits of a Supportive Community

- Spiritual Growth: A supportive community fosters spiritual growth by providing opportunities for worship, learning, and mutual encouragement.

- Emotional Well-being: The emotional support offered by a community can reduce stress, anxiety, and loneliness.

- Sense of Belonging: Being part of a community satisfies the human need for connection and belonging, enhancing overall life satisfaction.

- Collective Strength: A united community can accomplish more collectively than individuals working alone, addressing broader social and spiritual needs.

4.3.6 Relevance for Today

Building a supportive community is essential for contemporary believers. It teaches that:

- Reflecting God's Love: A supportive community reflects God's love and character, demonstrating His care and compassion to the world.

- Mutual Responsibility: Each member has a role in supporting and uplifting others, contributing to the well-being of the entire community.

- Holistic Health: A supportive community promotes holistic health—spiritual, emotional, and physical—enhancing overall quality of life.

Building a supportive community is foundational for fostering growth and helping individuals unlock their potential. By embracing biblical principles of love, unity, mutual care, hospitality, and encouragement, we can create communities that reflect God's character and nurture each member. Through practical steps and a commitment to genuine relationships, inclusivity, service, support, and encouragement, we can cultivate environments where individuals thrive and fulfill their God-given potential. The theological perspective on community offers profound insights and guidance for creating such supportive and transformative communities.

4.4 Empowering Through Education

Education is a powerful tool for empowerment and personal development. The Bible recognizes the importance of teaching and training, especially in the early stages of life. Proverbs 22:6 (NIV) states, "Start children off on the way they should go, and even when they are old they will not turn from it." This chapter explores the significance of education in developing potential, highlighting biblical teachings, and integrating psychological and philosophical perspectives on the role of education in empowerment.

4.4.1 Biblical Foundation for Education

The Bible underscores the importance of education and training in shaping individuals and communities.

The Role of Parents and Guardians: Deuteronomy 6:6-7 (NIV) instructs, "These commandments that I give you today are to be on your hearts. Impress them on your children. Talk about them when you sit at home and when you walk along the road, when you lie down and when you get up." The Hebrew term for impress, shanan (H8150), means to sharpen or teach diligently. This emphasizes the responsibility of parents and guardians to educate their children in God's ways.

Wisdom and Understanding: Proverbs 4:7 (NIV) declares, "The beginning of wisdom is this: Get wisdom. Though it cost all you have, get understanding." The Hebrew word for wisdom, chokmah (H2451), and understanding, biynah (H998), highlight the value of pursuing knowledge and insight.

Jesus as a Teacher: Jesus' ministry was marked by His role as a teacher. In Matthew 4:23 (NIV), it is recorded, "Jesus went throughout Galilee, teaching in their synagogues, proclaiming the good news of the kingdom, and healing every disease and sickness among the people." Jesus' teachings continue to influence and guide millions, emphasizing the transformative power of education.

4.4.2 The Impact of Education on Potential

Education has a profound impact on developing potential. It provides individuals with the knowledge, skills, and confidence to pursue their goals and contribute meaningfully to society.

Knowledge and Skills Development: Education equips individuals with essential knowledge and skills. Hosea 4:6 (NIV) warns, "My people are destroyed from lack of knowledge." The Hebrew word for knowledge, daath (H1847), signifies awareness and understanding, underscoring the importance of education in preventing destruction and fostering growth.

Character Formation: Education also plays a crucial role in shaping character. 2 Timothy 3:16-17 (NIV) states, "All Scripture is God-breathed and is useful for teaching, rebuking, correcting and training in righteousness, so that the servant of God may be thoroughly equipped for every good work." The Greek term for training, paideia (G3809), implies discipline and instruction aimed at moral and spiritual development.

Empowerment and Confidence: An educated individual is often more confident and empowered to take on leadership roles and make informed decisions. Daniel 1:17 (NIV) describes how God gave Daniel and his friends knowledge and understanding: "To these four young men God gave knowledge and understanding of all kinds of literature and learning. And Daniel could understand visions and dreams of all kinds." Their education empowered them to serve in influential positions in Babylon.

4.4.3 Psychological Perspective on Education

From a psychological standpoint, education is essential for cognitive and emotional development.

Cognitive Development: Jean Piaget's theory of cognitive development emphasizes the role of education in enhancing intellectual growth. Education stimulates critical thinking, problem-solving, and creativity, which are crucial for realizing potential.

Emotional and Social Development: Education also fosters emotional and social development. Erik Erikson's stages of psychosocial development highlight the importance of social interactions and education in forming a strong sense of identity and competence.

Self-Efficacy and Motivation: Albert Bandura's concept of self-efficacy demonstrates how education boosts individuals' belief in their abilities to succeed. Higher self-efficacy leads to greater motivation and persistence in achieving goals.

4.4.4 Philosophical Perspective on Education

Philosophers have long recognized the transformative power of education.

Plato and the Role of Education: In "The Republic," Plato advocates for education as a means to achieve justice and the ideal state. He emphasizes the importance of education in cultivating virtuous and knowledgeable citizens.

John Dewey and Experiential Learning: John Dewey, a prominent educational philosopher, argued for experiential learning, where education is an active and dynamic process. He believed that education should prepare individuals for participation in democratic society and personal fulfillment.

Paulo Freire and Empowerment: Paulo Freire's "Pedagogy of the Oppressed" highlights education as a tool for empowerment and liberation. He advocates for an educational approach that encourages critical thinking and active participation in social change.

4.4.5 Practical Steps for Empowering Through Education

1. Provide Access to Quality Education: Ensure that education is accessible and inclusive for all individuals, regardless of their background. Proverbs 2:6 (NIV) states, "For the Lord gives wisdom; from his mouth come knowledge and understanding."

2. Encourage Lifelong Learning: Promote the idea that education is a lifelong journey. Proverbs 9:9 (NIV) advises, "Instruct the wise and they will be wiser still; teach the righteous and they will add to their learning."

3. Integrate Faith and Learning: Combine spiritual teachings with academic education to provide a holistic learning experience. Colossians 3:16 (NIV) encourages, "Let the message of Christ dwell among you richly as you teach and admonish one another with all wisdom through psalms, hymns, and songs from the Spirit, singing to God with gratitude in your hearts."

4. Foster Critical Thinking and Creativity: Encourage critical thinking and creativity to help individuals solve problems and innovate. Romans 12:2 (NIV) states, "Do not conform to the pattern of this world, but be transformed by the renewing of your mind."

5. Support and Mentor Learners: Provide mentorship and support to guide learners in their educational journey. 2 Timothy 2:2 (NIV) instructs, "And the things you have heard

me say in the presence of many witnesses entrust to reliable people who will also be qualified to teach others."

4.4.6 The Benefits of Empowering Through Education

- Enhanced Personal Growth: Education fosters personal development and self-awareness, helping individuals realize their potential.

- Improved Economic Opportunities: Educated individuals have better employment prospects and can contribute to economic growth.

- Stronger Communities: Education promotes social cohesion and active citizenship, leading to stronger and more resilient communities.

- Informed Decision-Making: Education equips individuals with the knowledge and skills to make informed decisions and participate effectively in society.

4.4.7 Relevance for Today

Empowering through education is vital for contemporary society. It teaches that:

- Investing in Education: Investing in education is crucial for individual and societal progress.

- Lifelong Learning: Education should be seen as a continuous journey that extends beyond formal schooling.

- Holistic Approach: Integrating faith and learning can provide a comprehensive and fulfilling educational experience.

Empowering others through education is a vital component of developing potential and fostering growth. By providing opportunities for learning and integrating biblical principles, psychological insights, and philosophical perspectives, we can create environments that nurture and empower individuals. Through practical steps and a commitment to quality education, lifelong learning, and holistic development, we can help others reach their full potential and contribute meaningfully to society.

CHAPTER 05

THE LEGACY OF REALIZED POTENTIAL

5.1 Biblical Legacies

The legacies of biblical figures such as David, Solomon, and Paul provide powerful examples of how realizing one's potential can have a lasting impact. Their lives, marked by faith, leadership, and perseverance, continue to inspire and guide individuals in their spiritual journeys. This chapter explores the legacies of these key biblical figures, examining how their realized potential has shaped history and influenced countless generations.

5.1.1 The Legacy of David

David's Journey from Shepherd to King

David's story begins with humble beginnings as a shepherd boy and culminates in his reign as the King of Israel. His journey is a testament to God's ability to elevate the faithful and use them for great purposes. 1 Samuel 16:13 (NIV) records Samuel anointing David: "So Samuel took the horn of oil and anointed him in the presence of his brothers, and from that day on the Spirit of the Lord came powerfully upon David."

David's Courage and Faith

David's defeat of Goliath is one of the most iconic stories of courage and faith in the Bible. 1 Samuel 17:45-47 (NIV) highlights David's faith: "David said to the Philistine, 'You come against me with sword and spear and javelin, but I come against you in the name of the Lord Almighty... This day the Lord will deliver you into my hands.'"

David's Leadership and Heart for God

David's leadership was marked by his deep relationship with God. Despite his flaws, he was described as a man after God's own heart (Acts 13:22). His legacy includes the establishment of Jerusalem as the political and spiritual center of Israel, and his psalms continue to be a source of comfort and worship.

5.1.2 The Legacy of Solomon

Solomon's Wisdom

Solomon, David's son, is renowned for his wisdom. When God offered to grant him anything he wished, Solomon asked for wisdom to govern the people. 1 Kings 3:9 (NIV) records Solomon's request: "So give your servant a discerning heart to govern your people and to distinguish between right and wrong."

Solomon's Contributions to Literature

Solomon's wisdom is reflected in his contributions to biblical literature, including Proverbs, Ecclesiastes, and Song of Songs. Proverbs 1:7 (NIV) states, "The fear of the Lord is the beginning of knowledge, but fools despise wisdom and instruction." These writings continue to provide practical guidance and spiritual insights.

Solomon's Temple

One of Solomon's most significant legacies is the construction of the temple in Jerusalem. 1 Kings 6:1 (NIV) describes the commencement of this monumental project: "In the four hundred and eightieth year after the Israelites came out of Egypt, in the fourth year of Solomon's reign over Israel, in the month of Ziv, the second month, he began to build the temple of the Lord." The temple became the central place of worship for the Israelites and a symbol of God's presence among His people.

5.1.3 The Legacy of Paul

Paul's Transformation and Mission

Paul's legacy begins with his dramatic conversion on the road to Damascus. Acts 9:15-16 (NIV) records God's purpose for Paul: "But the Lord said to Ananias, 'Go! This man is my chosen instrument to proclaim my name to the Gentiles and their kings and to the people of Israel. I will show him how much he must suffer for my name.'" Paul's transformation from a persecutor of Christians to a devoted apostle underscores the power of God's grace.

Paul's Evangelistic Journeys

Paul's missionary journeys were instrumental in spreading Christianity throughout the Roman Empire. His travels, recorded in the Book of Acts, led to the establishment of numerous churches and the spread of the Gospel message far beyond Israel.

Paul's Epistles

Paul's letters to the early churches form a significant portion of the New Testament. These epistles address theological issues, provide practical advice, and encourage believers. Romans 12:1-2 (NIV) exhorts, "Therefore, I urge you, brothers and sisters, in view of God's mercy, to offer your bodies as a living sacrifice, holy and pleasing to God— this is your true and proper worship. Do not conform to the pattern of this world, but be transformed by the renewing of your mind." Paul's teachings continue to shape Christian doctrine and practice.

Comprehensive Commentary

1 Samuel 16:13: The anointing of David by Samuel signifies God's choice and empowerment for leadership. The Hebrew term for anoint, mashach (H4886), indicates consecration and divine selection.

1 Samuel 17:45-47: David's confrontation with Goliath underscores his faith and reliance on God's power. The term Lord Almighty, Yahweh Sabaoth (H3068 and H6635), emphasizes God's sovereignty and might.

Acts 13:22: David's designation as a man after God's own heart highlights his deep spiritual connection with God. The term heart, lebab (H3824), refers to the inner being and character.

1 Kings 3:9: Solomon's request for a discerning heart illustrates his prioritization of wisdom over wealth or power. The term discerning heart, leb shomea (H3824 and H8085), emphasizes the need for understanding and discernment.

Proverbs 1:7: The fear of the Lord as the foundation of knowledge underscores the importance of a reverent relationship with God. The term fear, yirah (H3374), denotes awe and respect.

1 Kings 6:1: The construction of the temple signifies a central place of worship and God's dwelling among His people. The term temple, bayith (H1004), denotes a house or dwelling place.

Acts 9:15-16: Paul's divine commissioning highlights God's purpose and plan for his life. The term chosen instrument, skeuos ekloges (G4632 and G1589), signifies selection for a specific purpose.

Romans 12:1-2: Paul's exhortation to live as a living sacrifice underscores the call to holiness and transformation. The term renewing of your mind, anakainosis nous (G342 and G3563), emphasizes the process of spiritual renewal.

5.1.4 Practical Lessons from Biblical Legacies

1. Faith and Obedience: The legacies of David, Solomon, and Paul highlight the importance of faith and obedience to God's calling. Hebrews 11:1 (NIV) defines faith as "confidence in what we hope for and assurance about what we do not see."

2. Wisdom and Understanding: Pursuing wisdom and understanding, as exemplified by Solomon, is crucial for personal and communal growth. James 1:5 (NIV) advises, "If any of you lacks wisdom, you should ask God, who gives generously to all without finding fault, and it will be given to you."

3. Transformation and Mission: Paul's life demonstrates the power of transformation and the importance of living out God's mission. 2 Corinthians 5:17 (NIV) states, "Therefore, if anyone is in Christ, the new creation has come: The old has gone, the new is here!"

4. Legacy of Service: All three figures left legacies of service to God and others, emphasizing the impact of dedicating one's life to a higher purpose. Mark 10:45 (NIV) reflects this: "For even the Son of Man did not come to be served, but to serve, and to give his life as a ransom for many."

5.1.5 Relevance for Today

The legacies of David, Solomon, and Paul remain profoundly relevant for contemporary believers. They teach that:

- God Uses Imperfect People: Despite their flaws, these figures were used mightily by God, demonstrating that God can use anyone who is willing and faithful.

- The Importance of Godly Leadership: Effective and godly leadership can have a lasting impact on communities and future generations.

- The Power of Faith and Wisdom: Faith in God and the pursuit of wisdom are foundational for achieving one's potential and leaving a meaningful legacy.

The legacies of biblical figures such as David, Solomon, and Paul illustrate the lasting impact of realizing one's potential. Their stories, marked by faith, wisdom, and service, continue to inspire and guide individuals in their spiritual journeys. By examining their lives through comprehensive biblical teachings and practical lessons, we gain deeper insights into the principles and practices that contribute to a lasting legacy. Their examples encourage us to live faithfully, pursue wisdom, and dedicate our lives to serving God and others.

5.2 Historical Legacies

Throughout history, many individuals have left enduring legacies by recognizing and actualizing their potential. Figures such as Abraham Lincoln, Mother Teresa, and Nelson Mandela have profoundly influenced society through their contributions. This chapter explores their lives and legacies, illustrating how their actions and achievements continue to inspire and guide us today.

5.2.1 The Legacy of Abraham Lincoln

Early Life and Struggles

Abraham Lincoln, born into humble beginnings, faced numerous obstacles on his path to the presidency. His early life was marked by poverty, limited formal education, and personal loss. However, his determination and self-education laid the foundation for his future leadership.

Leadership During the Civil War

As the 16th President of the United States, Lincoln's leadership during the Civil War was pivotal in preserving the Union and abolishing slavery. His commitment to justice and equality is epitomized in the Emancipation Proclamation, issued on January 1, 1863, which declared the freedom of all enslaved people in Confederate-held territory.

Gettysburg Address

One of Lincoln's most famous speeches, the Gettysburg Address, delivered on November 19, 1863, redefined the purpose of the war and underscored the principles of liberty and equality. His words, "that this nation, under God, shall have a new birth of freedom—and that government of the people, by the people, for the people, shall not perish from the earth," continue to resonate as a testament to democratic ideals.

Assassination and Enduring Legacy

Lincoln's assassination on April 14, 1865, cut short his life but not his legacy. His leadership, vision for equality, and efforts to heal a divided nation have left an indelible mark on American history and continue to inspire leaders worldwide.

5.2.2 The Legacy of Mother Teresa

Early Life and Calling

Mother Teresa, born Anjezë Gonxhe Bojaxhiu in 1910 in Macedonia, felt a calling to serve the poor at a young age. She joined the Sisters of Loreto at 18 and moved to India, where she taught at a convent school.

Founding the Missionaries of Charity

In 1948, Mother Teresa left the convent to live among the poor in the slums of Calcutta. She founded the Missionaries of Charity in 1950, with a mission to care for "the hungry, the naked, the homeless, the crippled, the blind, the lepers, all those people who feel unwanted, unloved, uncared for throughout society."

Global Impact and Recognition

Mother Teresa's work garnered international recognition and inspired countless individuals to engage in humanitarian efforts. She received numerous awards, including the Nobel Peace Prize in 1979. Her famous words, "Not all of us can do great things. But we can do small things with great love," encapsulate her philosophy of service.

Canonization and Continued Influence

Mother Teresa was canonized as Saint Teresa of Calcutta in 2016, affirming her enduring influence. Her legacy of compassion, selfless service, and dedication to the marginalized continues to inspire individuals and organizations worldwide to work towards alleviating poverty and suffering.

5.2.3 The Legacy of Nelson Mandela

Early Life and Anti-Apartheid Activism

Nelson Mandela, born in 1918 in South Africa, became a central figure in the struggle against apartheid. As a member of the African National Congress (ANC), he advocated for nonviolent resistance against racial segregation. Mandela's activism led to his imprisonment for 27 years, during which he became a symbol of resistance and hope.

Leadership and Reconciliation

Upon his release in 1990, Mandela played a crucial role in the negotiations to end apartheid. He was elected as South Africa's first black president in 1994, marking a significant transition towards democracy. His leadership emphasized reconciliation and nation-building, striving to heal the divisions caused by decades of institutionalized racism.

Truth and Reconciliation Commission

Mandela established the Truth and Reconciliation Commission (TRC) to address the human rights violations that occurred during apartheid. The TRC's work was pivotal in fostering national healing and setting a precedent for addressing historical injustices through truth and forgiveness.

Global Influence and Legacy

Nelson Mandela's legacy extends beyond South Africa. His commitment to justice, equality, and human rights has inspired global movements for social justice and democracy. Mandela's vision and perseverance continue to serve as a beacon of hope and a model for leadership in the pursuit of a just and equitable society.

Comprehensive Commentary

Abraham Lincoln: Lincoln's leadership during one of the most tumultuous times in American history showcases the power of perseverance and moral conviction. His ability to navigate the complexities of the Civil War and his dedication to the principles of liberty and equality have left a lasting legacy.

Mother Teresa: Mother Teresa's life exemplifies the transformative power of compassion and service. Her dedication to the poorest of the poor, despite the challenges, underscores the impact of selfless love and humility. Her legacy continues to inspire humanitarian efforts worldwide.

Nelson Mandela: Mandela's legacy is a testament to the strength of resilience and the power of forgiveness. His commitment to justice and reconciliation, even after decades of imprisonment, demonstrates the potential for individual and collective transformation. His influence continues to inspire movements for social justice and human rights globally.

5.2.4 Practical Lessons from Historical Legacies

1. Perseverance in the Face of Adversity: The lives of Lincoln, Mother Teresa, and Mandela highlight the importance of perseverance. James 1:12 (NIV) states, "Blessed is the one who perseveres under trial because, having stood the test, that person will receive the crown of life that the Lord has promised to those who love him."

2. Commitment to Justice and Equality: Their legacies underscore the significance of fighting for justice and equality. Micah 6:8 (NIV) exhorts, "He has shown you, O mortal, what is good. And what does the Lord require of you? To act justly and to love mercy and to walk humbly with your God."

3. Service to Others: Mother Teresa's life teaches the profound impact of serving others with love. Matthew 20:28 (NIV) reflects this: "Just as the Son of Man did not come to be served, but to serve, and to give his life as a ransom for many."

4. Reconciliation and Forgiveness: Mandela's efforts towards reconciliation highlight the power of forgiveness in healing divisions. Ephesians 4:32 (NIV) advises, "Be kind and compassionate to one another, forgiving each other, just as in Christ God forgave you."

5.2.5 Relevance for Today

The legacies of Abraham Lincoln, Mother Teresa, and Nelson Mandela remain profoundly relevant for contemporary society. They teach that:

- Leadership with Integrity: Effective leadership is rooted in integrity, moral conviction, and a commitment to justice.

- Compassionate Service: Selfless service to others can transform lives and communities.

- Resilience and Hope: Perseverance in the face of adversity can lead to significant and lasting change.

The historical legacies of Abraham Lincoln, Mother Teresa, and Nelson Mandela illustrate the profound influence of recognizing and actualizing one's potential. Their lives, marked by leadership, service, and resilience, continue to inspire and guide individuals and societies. By examining their contributions and the principles they embodied, we gain deeper insights into the impact of realized potential and the enduring power of living with purpose and conviction.

5.3 Your Legacy

Each individual possesses the potential to leave a lasting legacy. By embracing our God-given abilities and striving to fulfill our purpose, we contribute to a better world and inspire future generations. This chapter explores how you can build and leave a meaningful legacy through your actions, values, and impact on others. By examining biblical principles, personal development strategies, and practical steps, we can understand how to shape a legacy that honors God and benefits humanity.

5.3.1 Understanding Legacy

A legacy is the lasting impact one leaves on the world, reflected in the lives they touch, the values they uphold, and the contributions they make. Proverbs 13:22 (NIV) states, "A good person leaves an inheritance for their children's children, but a sinner's wealth is stored up for the righteous." The term inheritance, nachalah (H5159), encompasses more than material wealth; it includes the imparting of values, wisdom, and character.

5.3.2 Embracing Your God-Given Abilities

Recognizing Your Gifts

Every individual has unique gifts and talents bestowed by God. Romans 12:6-8 (NIV) encourages, "We have different gifts, according to the grace given to each of us. If your gift is prophesying, then prophesy in accordance with your faith; if it is serving, then serve; if it is teaching, then teach; if it is to encourage, then give encouragement; if it is giving, then give generously; if it is to lead, do it diligently; if it is to show mercy, do it cheerfully." Recognizing and utilizing these gifts is the first step toward building a lasting legacy.

Developing Your Skills

Embracing your God-given abilities involves continuous development. Proverbs 22:29 (NIV) states, "Do you see someone skilled in their work? They will serve before kings; they will not serve before officials of low rank." The Hebrew word for skilled, mahir (H4106), denotes proficiency and excellence. Investing time and effort in honing your skills enhances your capacity to make a significant impact.

5.3.3 Striving to Fulfill Your Purpose

Seeking God's Guidance

Fulfilling your purpose requires seeking God's guidance. Proverbs 3:5-6 (NIV) advises, "Trust in the Lord with all your heart and lean not on your own understanding; in all your ways submit to him, and he will make your paths straight." The term submit, yada (H3045), means to acknowledge or recognize. Acknowledging God in all your endeavors ensures alignment with His will.

Living with Intentionality

Living intentionally involves making conscious decisions that reflect your values and goals. Ephesians 5:15-17 (NIV) encourages, "Be very careful, then, how you live— not as unwise but as wise, making the most of every opportunity, because the days are evil. Therefore do not be foolish, but understand what the Lord's will is." Intentional living maximizes your impact and helps you stay focused on your divine purpose.

5.3.4 Building a Legacy through Relationships

Investing in Others

Building a legacy often involves investing in the lives of others. 2 Timothy 2:2 (NIV) states, "And the things you have heard me say in the presence of many witnesses entrust to reliable people who will also be qualified to teach others." Mentorship, encouragement, and support create a ripple effect that extends your influence across generations.

Demonstrating Love and Compassion

Jesus' command in John 13:34-35 (NIV) highlights the importance of love: "A new command I give you: Love one another. As I have loved you, so you must love one another. By this everyone will know that you are my disciples, if you love one another." The Greek word for love, agape (G26), signifies selfless, unconditional love. Demonstrating love and compassion leaves a powerful and enduring legacy.

5.3.5 Leaving a Legacy of Integrity and Faith

Upholding Integrity

Integrity is foundational to a lasting legacy. Proverbs 10:9 (NIV) asserts, "Whoever walks in integrity walks securely, but whoever takes crooked paths will be found out."

The term integrity, tom (H8537), denotes completeness and moral soundness. Upholding integrity in your actions builds trust and respect, influencing others positively.

Living Out Your Faith

Living out your faith involves being a witness to God's love and truth in every aspect of life. Matthew 5:14-16 (NIV) declares, "You are the light of the world. A town built on a hill cannot be hidden. Neither do people light a lamp and put it under a bowl. Instead, they put it on its stand, and it gives light to everyone in the house. In the same way, let your light shine before others, that they may see your good deeds and glorify your Father in heaven." Being a light to others leaves an indelible mark that points them to God.

5.3.6 Practical Steps to Build Your Legacy

1. Identify Your Values and Goals: Clearly define what you stand for and what you aim to achieve. Psalm 37:4 (NIV) encourages, "Take delight in the Lord, and he will give you the desires of your heart."

2. Engage in Lifelong Learning: Continuously seek knowledge and growth. Proverbs 1:5 (NIV) states, "Let the wise listen and add to their learning, and let the discerning get guidance."

3. Serve and Give Generously: Make service and generosity central to your life. Acts 20:35 (NIV) quotes Jesus, "It is more blessed to give than to receive."

4. Mentor and Empower Others: Invest time in mentoring and empowering others. Proverbs 27:17 (NIV) asserts, "As iron sharpens iron, so one person sharpens another."

5. Reflect and Adjust: Regularly reflect on your progress and make necessary adjustments. Lamentations 3:40 (NIV) advises, "Let us examine our ways and test them, and let us return to the Lord."

5.3.7 Relevance for Today

Building a legacy is essential for contemporary believers. It teaches that:

- Purposeful Living: Living with purpose and intentionality maximizes your impact on the world.

- Influence Through Relationships: Investing in relationships and demonstrating love creates a lasting influence.

- Integrity and Faith: Upholding integrity and living out your faith leave an enduring mark that honors God and inspires others.

Each individual has the potential to leave a lasting legacy. By embracing our God-given abilities, striving to fulfill our purpose, and investing in others, we can build a legacy that reflects God's love and contributes to a better world. Through practical steps and a commitment to integrity, faith, and intentional living, we can shape a legacy that honors God and inspires future generations. As we reflect on the lives of biblical and historical figures, let us be encouraged to pursue our potential and leave a legacy that glorifies God.

CONCLUSION

Understanding and unlocking our potential is a transformative journey that requires faith, perseverance, and a willingness to embrace our unique gifts. This journey is not just about personal growth but also about making a meaningful impact in the world, leaving a legacy that reflects God's love and purpose for our lives.

Embracing Faith and Perseverance

Faith is the cornerstone of realizing our potential. It involves trusting in God's plan, even when the path is unclear. Hebrews 11:1 (NIV) defines faith as "confidence in what we hope for and assurance about what we do not see." This confidence empowers us to move forward, knowing that God is with us every step of the way. Perseverance, as highlighted in James 1:12 (NIV), is also crucial: "Blessed is the one who perseveres under trial because, having stood the test, that person will receive the crown of life that the Lord has promised to those who love him." Our journey is marked by challenges, but through faith and perseverance, we can overcome obstacles and continue striving towards our goals.

Utilizing Our Unique Gifts

Each of us is endowed with unique gifts and talents. Recognizing and utilizing these gifts is essential for fulfilling our potential. Romans 12:6-8 (NIV) reminds us, "We have different gifts, according to the grace given to each of us." By identifying our strengths and developing our skills, we can make significant contributions to our communities and the world. This process of self-discovery and continuous growth enables us to become the best versions of ourselves, reflecting God's creativity and purpose.

Drawing Inspiration from Biblical and Historical Examples

The lives of biblical figures such as David, Solomon, and Paul, as well as historical figures like Abraham Lincoln, Mother Teresa, and Nelson Mandela, provide powerful examples of realized potential. These individuals, through their faith, wisdom, and perseverance, have left lasting legacies that continue to inspire and guide us. Their stories illustrate that realizing one's potential is not just about personal achievement but about serving others, advocating for justice, and living out God's calling.

Building a Supportive Community

A supportive community plays a crucial role in helping us realize our potential. Hebrews 10:24-25 (NIV) urges us to "spur one another on toward love and good deeds, not giving up meeting together... but encouraging one another." Surrounding ourselves with a community of faith provides the encouragement, accountability, and support we need to grow and thrive. By investing in others, mentoring, and fostering genuine relationships, we can build communities that nurture and empower individuals to reach their full potential.

Leaving a Lasting Legacy

Our journey of realizing potential is ultimately about leaving a legacy that honors God and benefits future generations. Proverbs 13:22 (NIV) states, "A good person leaves an inheritance for their children's children." This inheritance goes beyond material wealth to include the values, wisdom, and faith we impart to others. By living with integrity, serving others, and staying true to our purpose, we can create a lasting impact that inspires and guides those who come after us.

Final Thoughts

The journey to understanding and unlocking our potential is an ongoing process that requires dedication and a willingness to grow. By embracing faith, recognizing and developing our unique gifts, drawing inspiration from exemplary figures, and building supportive communities, we can fulfill our God-given potential. This journey is not just about personal fulfillment but about making a meaningful impact in the world and leaving a legacy that glorifies God.

As we conclude this exploration of potential, let us be reminded of Philippians 4:13 (NIV): "I can do all this through him who gives me strength." With God's guidance and strength, we can overcome any obstacle, achieve our goals, and contribute to a better world. May we continue to seek His wisdom and walk in His purpose, knowing that our lives have the power to inspire and transform future generations.

Dr. Maxwell Shimba

APPENDIX A, B, C, AND D

Appendix A: Key Biblical Verses on Potential and Legacy

Faith and Perseverance

- Hebrews 11:1 (NIV): "Now faith is confidence in what we hope for and assurance about what we do not see."

- James 1:12 (NIV): "Blessed is the one who perseveres under trial because, having stood the test, that person will receive the crown of life that the Lord has promised to those who love him."

Unique Gifts and Talents

- Romans 12:6-8 (NIV): "We have different gifts, according to the grace given to each of us. If your gift is prophesying, then prophesy in accordance with your faith; if it is serving, then serve; if it is teaching, then teach; if it is to encourage, then give encouragement; if it is giving, then give generously; if it is to lead, do it diligently; if it is to show mercy, do it cheerfully."

- Proverbs 22:29 (NIV): "Do you see someone skilled in their work? They will serve before kings; they will not serve before officials of low rank."

Building Community and Supporting Others

- Hebrews 10:24-25 (NIV): "And let us consider how we may spur one another on toward love and good deeds, not giving up meeting together, as some are in the habit of doing, but encouraging one another—and all the more as you see the Day approaching."

- 2 Timothy 2:2 (NIV): "And the things you have heard me say in the presence of many witnesses entrust to reliable people who will also be qualified to teach others."

Living with Integrity and Faith

- Proverbs 10:9 (NIV): "Whoever walks in integrity walks securely, but whoever takes crooked paths will be found out."

- Matthew 5:14-16 (NIV): "You are the light of the world. A town built on a hill cannot be hidden. Neither do people light a lamp and put it under a bowl. Instead, they put it on its stand, and it gives light to everyone in the house. In the same way, let your light shine before others, that they may see your good deeds and glorify your Father in heaven."

Leaving a Legacy

- Proverbs 13:22 (NIV): "A good person leaves an inheritance for their children's children, but a sinner's wealth is stored up for the righteous."

- Philippians 4:13 (NIV): "I can do all this through him who gives me strength."

Appendix B: Key Historical Figures and Their Contributions

Abraham Lincoln

- Early Life and Struggles: Overcoming poverty and limited education.

- Leadership During the Civil War: Preservation of the Union and the Emancipation Proclamation.

- Gettysburg Address: Reaffirmation of democratic principles.

- Assassination and Legacy: Enduring impact on American history and democratic ideals.

Mother Teresa

- Early Life and Calling: Dedication to serving the poor.

- Missionaries of Charity: Founding and expanding the order to serve the marginalized.

- Global Impact and Recognition: Nobel Peace Prize and international humanitarian efforts.

- Canonization: Recognition as Saint Teresa of Calcutta.

Nelson Mandela

- Anti-Apartheid Activism: Leading the struggle against racial segregation.

- Imprisonment and Symbol of Hope: 27 years of imprisonment and global symbol of resistance.

- Leadership and Reconciliation: Ending apartheid and promoting national healing.

- Global Influence and Legacy: Inspiration for social justice and human rights movements.

Appendix C: Practical Steps for Realizing Potential

Identify Your Values and Goals

- Define what you stand for and aim to achieve.

- Reflect on Psalm 37:4 (NIV): "Take delight in the Lord, and he will give you the desires of your heart."

Engage in Lifelong Learning

- Continuously seek knowledge and growth.

- Proverbs 1:5 (NIV): "Let the wise listen and add to their learning, and let the discerning get guidance."

Serve and Give Generously

- Make service and generosity central to your life.

- Acts 20:35 (NIV): "It is more blessed to give than to receive."

Mentor and Empower Others

- Invest time in mentoring and empowering others.

- Proverbs 27:17 (NIV): "As iron sharpens iron, so one person sharpens another."

Reflect and Adjust

- Regularly reflect on your progress and make necessary adjustments.

- Lamentations 3:40 (NIV): "Let us examine our ways and test them, and let us return to the Lord."

Appendix D: Reflective Questions for Personal Growth

Self-Assessment

1. What are my unique gifts and talents?

2. How am I currently using my gifts to serve others?

3. What are my core values, and how do they shape my actions?

Goal Setting

1. What are my short-term and long-term goals?

2. How can I align my goals with God's purpose for my life?

3. What steps can I take today to move closer to my goals?

Community Engagement

1. How can I contribute to building a supportive community?

2. Who can I mentor or support in their journey of realizing potential?

3. How can I demonstrate love and compassion in my daily interactions?

Legacy Building

1. What kind of legacy do I want to leave?

2. How can I live with integrity and faith in all aspects of my life?

3. What steps can I take to ensure my actions have a positive impact on future generations?

Dr. Maxwell Shimba